T0330460

Europe Incorporated

Europe Incorporated

The New Challenge

Gianni Montezemolo
A.T. Kearney

JOHN WILEY & SONS, LTD
Chichester · New York · Weinheim · Brisbane · Singapore · Toronto

Published by John Wiley & Sons Ltd,
Baffins Lane, Chichester,
West Sussex PO19 1UD, England

National 01243 779777
International (+44) 1243 779777
e-mail (for orders and customer service enquiries): cs-books@wiley.co.uk
Visit our Home Page on http://www.wiley.co.uk
or http://www.wiley.com

Other Wiley Editorial Offices

John Wiley & Sons, Inc., 605 Third Avenue,
New York, NY 10158-0012, USA

WILEY-VCH GmbH, Pappelallee 3,
D-69469 Weinheim, Germany

Jacaranda Wiley Ltd, 33 Park Road, Milton,
Queensland 4064, Australia

John Wiley & Sons (Asia) Pte Ltd, 2 Clementi Loop #02-01,
Jin Xing Distripark, Singapore 129809

John Wiley & Sons (Canada) Ltd, 22 Worcester Road,
Rexdale, Ontario M9W 1L1, Canada

Library of Congress Cataloging-in-Publication Data

Montezemolo, Gianni.
Europe Incorporated/Gianni Montezemolo.
p. cm.
Includes bibliographical references and index.
ISBN 0–471–62388–1 (case : alk. paper)
1. Corporations — Europe. 2. Industrial management — Europe.
I. Title.
HD2844.M66 1999
658′. 049′ 094 — dc21 99–35169
CIP

British Library Cataloguing in Publication Data

A catalogue record for this book is available from the British Library

ISBN 0-471-623881

Typeset in Garamond 11/13pt by The Midlands Book Typesetting Company, Loughborough.
Printed and bound by Antony Rowe Ltd, Eastbourne

Contents

Foreword

"One Europe." There is no more magical phrase in international commerce. With the birth of the euro and the convergence of 15 nation-markets, every company on the continent is eagerly looking at this brave new geography. Timing is perfect. Most corporations have already expended considerable resources on globalization. The emerging of new markets (in Asia, for example) has demanded swift incisive response. Those companies who have made that investment stand to benefit over the next decade.

But the spotlight has swung back toward Europe once more. In *Europe, Incorporated: The New Challenge*, Gianni Montezemolo maintains that the global economy's new center of gravity will be Europe. He convincingly argues that those companies that refocus on the New Europe stand to gain dramatically over the near and longer term. Montezemolo's provocative message to CEOs and the companies they run is that they need to develop a vision of how Europe will expand, change, develop and become integrated over the next decades. They should prepare their organizations to confront these changes.

Concisely and clearly, the author dissects the emerging pan-European market and the distinctly different markets within it. He then moves beyond analysis. He offers a new European model useful to companies grounded in tradition, yet eager to embrace the changes that have begun to transform products and processes across the globe. New borders and boundaries define new worlds. To share in what he calls the "coming European hegemony", Montezemolo insists that all companies — European, American, Asian — must change approaches to everything from strategy, innovation, branding and R&D to distribution, pricing, sourcing, training, and recruiting.

Europe Incorporated: The New Challenge offers fresh, clear insights into where Europe is heading and what to do about it. Anyone with an interest in the Europe of tomorrow will profit from reading these pages.

George Fisher
Chairman and CEO Kodak

Acknowledgements

I owe a deep debt of gratitude to the chief executives of the following companies, who gave me hours of their precious time to talk about the issues addressed in this book: Benetton, Bestfoods, Cadbury-Schweppes, Case, Danone, Diageo, Fiat, Fort James, Freudenberg, Gillette, Heinz, Henkel, Iveco, Johnson & Johnson, Kimberly-Clark, Kodak, Mars, Max Mara, McCormick, Merloni, Nestlé, Pepsi Cola, Philips, Procter & Gamble, Quest, Sara Lee, SC Johnson Wax, Seagram, Sony, Unilever, Vorwerk and Zucchi/Bassetti.

I am also particularly indebted to my senior editors Tom Lloyd and Marita van Oldenburgh, who helped greatly with writing and re-writing the manuscript.

Introduction

In 1968, the distinguished French journalist, Jean-Jacques Servan-Schreiber caused quite a stir in European political and industrial circles, with his book, *Le Defi Americain* (*The American Challenge*). He argued that American industry, technology and culture were poised to dominate a gravely weakened Europe and warned, "we are simply letting European industry be … destroyed by the superior power of American corporations." The knight in shining armor, who had liberated Europe from the Nazi tyranny had become, if not an enemy, at least a predatory superpower bent on economic and cultural conquest. American corporations, with their enormous economies of scale in their home market, did indeed come to dominate the business world, but now the wheel has turned full circle. Over the next two decades or so the world economy's center of gravity will shift from North America and return to its birthplace in Europe. It is 'Le Defi Européen' that now confronts America and the rest of the business world.

The faltering of Asia's economies and the rapid economic integration of the European Union (EU) are accelerating the trend, but it is to the emergence of a peaceful Europe that future historians will attribute the shift in the balance of global economic power at the beginning of the 21st century. Centuries of war and the constant fear of war had prevented the emergence of an integrated European economy. The collapse of the Berlin Wall in 1989 started a spontaneous European economic and cultural fusion that has little directly to do with politics, or government, and is beginning to give real substance to the economic potential of 600 million well-educated and peacefully co-existing Europeans. Poland, Hungary and the Czech Republic are full voting members of NATO, and within a few years, they, along with Estonia and Slovenia, will be members of the EU, too. They are already trading mostly with their western neighbors, and have thereby increased the size of Europe's market to 450 million consumers, almost twice as large as the market of the USA. Russia, Belarus and Ukraine, with another 210 million consumers are following rapidly in the westernization process.

Nestlé's Chief Executive Officer (CEO), Peter Brabeck-Letmathe, believes the implications of Europe's historic economic enlargement are not confined to Europe. "The crumbling of the Berlin Wall has had dramatic effects on the market, and well beyond Europe. It has sparked a series of free trade initiatives that have brought some two billion new consumers into the world economy. These are not only consumers of our products, they are also suppliers of cheaper labor, with an obvious dampening effect on the inflationary pressures in the western world, and consequently on the spending expectations of western consumers." The emergence of greater Europe is the single most important business issue facing multinational firms, on the eve of the millennium. CEOs must widen their horizons, embrace the emergence of greater Europe, re-shape their organizations to reflect new priorities, and re-organize their operations to exploit low-cost manufacturing and sourcing opportunities to capture the synergies offered by a larger, more integrated Europe.

Western companies are already looking eastwards for their new manufacturing sites. Foreign direct investment in Hungary, Poland and the Czech Republic more than doubled in 1995, to a cumulative total of over €21 billion since 1990, and *The Economist* Intelligence Unit expects this to rise to €50 billion over the next five years. Appropriate production strategies range from outsourcing and licensing, to joint ventures and 100% foreign-owned plants, acquired or established on greenfield sites.

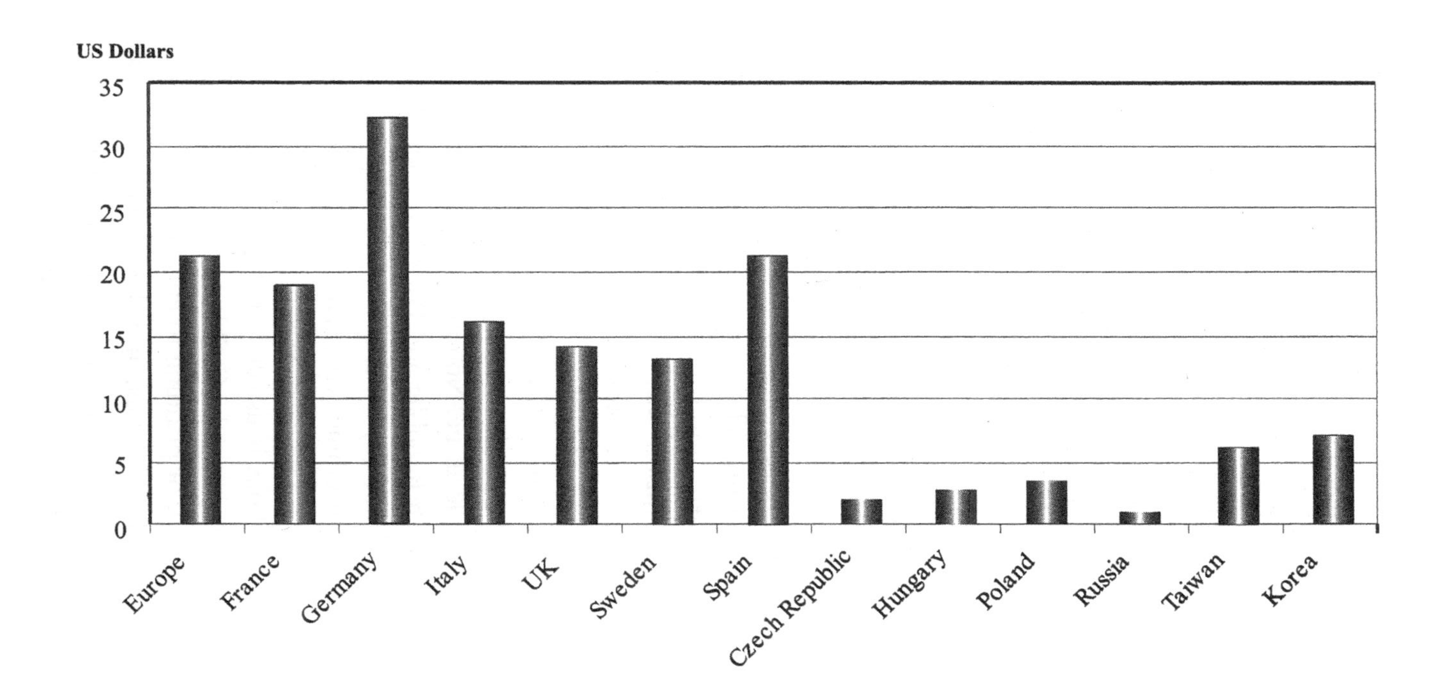

Source: Morgan Stanley

Figure 1.1 Hourly compensation in manufacturing (1995)

The case for putting manufacturing capacity in eastern Europe is compelling for all companies operating global sourcing and just-in-time supply chains. Manufacturing labor costs are comparable to those on the Pacific Rim (see Figure 1.1), the infrastructures are frequently better, and eastern Europe is closer to western Europe. The Iron Curtain distorted our geographical perceptions, and made it easy to forget that Prague is well to the west of Vienna. In the auto industry, General Motors has allocated $800 million for investments to the region, Volkswagen has developed budget models at its Czech subsidiary, Skoda, to take on lower-cost Asian competitors and Toyota plans to assemble cars in eastern Europe. The quality of eastern European products is growing steadily: in a recent UK survey of car owners, Skoda's new model came first out of 100 in customer satisfaction.

It is not just capital flows that are giving a new coherence to the greater European economy. The tastes of eastern and central Europeans for western goods have already been amply demonstrated. At SC Johnson Wax, volumes in Poland after only seven years in the market were similar to those in Spain, a similar sized market, where the company had been operating very successfully for 30 years. And 30% of Nestlé's European chocolate sales are now in central and eastern Europe. Nor is this region as risky, these days, as people allege. No one questions the need to be in Greece, but the Czech Republic and Poland are both larger (in terms of population), and enjoy lower risk ratings. They are socially homogeneous, free from ethnic strife, and as vociferous in their desires to join the EU, as Hungary, Slovenia and the Baltic States. Eastern Europe, as a whole, is usually rated safer by business risk assessors than Latin America or the Caribbean. The imperatives now, for companies already in, or planning to enter eastern Europe, are to take stock, establish priorities, and decide how to organize themselves. However, before firms can respond appropriately to this challenge, they need a vision of how Europe will expand, change shape, develop and become integrated over the next decade.

This book is designed to help CEOs develop such a vision. The six chapters of Part 1—'A vision of greater Europe'—are designed to help CEOs address the organizational design issues raised by the emergence of greater Europe. Chapter 1 explains why Europe, rather than Asia, is destined to be the next economic superpower, why economic dominance is important for companies, and why Americans will find it particularly hard to adapt to the new balance of world economic power. Chapter 2 considers the organizational design options for companies and introduces a tool that will help CEOs develop more appropriate frameworks for their European operations. Chapters 3 to 6 examine the components of this new model of Europe in more detail.

The five chapters of Part 2—'Managing greater Europe'—are designed to help CEOs address the major business issues of the day, within the context of the geographical framework described in Part 1. They suggest ways in which companies can exploit the new economies of scale and scope greater Europe offers. Chapter 7 discusses 'market entry' issues and proposes a new organizational model for greater Europe. Chapter 8 emphasizes the importance of innovation and suggests how European R&D might be organized. Chapter 9 addresses the vexed issues of brands and prices. Chapter 10 sketches out a blueprint for a supply chain for greater Europe. Chapter 11 considers the crucial, often neglected administrative implications of Europe's expansion, and how CEOs might go about building pan-European management teams.

Europe has entered a period of fundamental cultural and economic change, and all companies (European, American and Asian) that wish to be part of this emerging economic superpower must change themselves in equally fundamental ways.

Part 1

A Vision of Greater Europe

1
Europe's Second Coming

Ever since Marco Polo published his account of his travels at the beginning of the 14th century, westerners have been fascinated by the orient, and very aware of its latent military and economic power. "Let China sleep," Napoleon said, "for when she awakes the world will tremble." Over the past two decades, most of the world's multinational companies have been similarly dazzled by the potential of Asian markets, and allowed hopes of fabulous profits to triumph constantly over the experience of losses and failed alliances. In explaining their persistence, CEOs talk of the 'first mover advantage' and of how hard and expensive it is to establish your products in an economy after it has taken off. Asia will awake and, when it does, the business world will tremble because it will be the locomotive economy, and all of us will feel the power of its driving wheels. The question is: when?

The first locomotive economy was Great Britain, the birthplace of industry itself. The British Industrial Revolution, the first such revolution, was a major discontinuity in global economic development and was, for half a century, the only example of its kind. Foreigners coveted Britain's power and wealth, and tried hard to understand its causes, but it took them a long time to catch up. By the end of the 19th century, France and the recently unified Germany were close behind, however, and Europe rather than merely England had become the dominant economic power in a rapidly industrializing world.

According to Lester Thurow, "Whichever [economic power] pulls ahead, is apt to stay ahead ... [because it builds] the world's best ... economic system." But economic leads can be lost, and Europe's dominance was shattered by war: by the mid-20th century, the baton of world economic dominance had passed to the USA. America had a unique advantage: an enormous, single currency market consisting of at least four times as many consumers as the largest European country and twice as many as Japan, which offered its companies far greater economies of scale than those available in other industrialized economies.

Until recently, it was generally assumed that Japan's post-war economic miracle heralded another westward shift in the leadership of economic power from the USA to Asia, and that the fulfillment of the predictions of Napoleon and those multinational CEOs was imminent. For the moment, however, Asia's economic awakening is on hold. The Japanese economic system has proved flawed and the economic development of China and India has proceeded less quickly than expected. There is little doubt that, by the mid-21st century, Asia will dominate the world economy, but the signs are that, in the meantime, the baton will move from USA to Europe. Over the next two decades, an enlarged, economically integrated Europe will once again be the center of the economic world.

Some may argue that the North American Free Trade Area (NAFTA), incorporating the USA, Canada and Mexico, will ensure that America will continue to dominate the business world, because it is the beginning of the integration of north and south America. But NAFTA is not yet even a common market, because only goods, not people, can move freely within it. When it comes to continental integration, Europeans have two crucial advantages over Americans: a 40-year head-start and a long history of dealing with each other, economically and culturally, in many languages. They are much more likely than the Americans to make a success of a single market with diverse ethnic components. Moreover, the headline figures leave little room for doubt about Europe's second economic coming. It is almost as populous as NAFTA and Latin America combined, its €7.6 trillion a year of gross national product (GNP) is already greater than that of the Americas (see Figure 1.2), and it is likely to grow faster in the next two decades, as the well-educated people of eastern Europe adopt western business practices and technology, and seek to achieve western European standards of living.

THE SIGNIFICANCE OF DOMINANCE

World economic dominance is not simply a matter of statistics. The location of the dominant trading bloc is of great significance for business, because it establishes a pre-eminent economic system, and a set of rules, practices, conventions and standards with which any company with global aspirations must comply. Companies outside the pre-eminent system that want to deal with it need to adopt its standards. British dominance in the 19th century established sterling as the world's reserve currency, and led to the adoption of imperial measurement systems all over the world. In the middle of the 20th century the US dollar replaced sterling as the world's reserve currency, but the Americans inherited their measurement systems from Britain and still cling to inches, gallons and pounds. In Europe even reluctant Europeans, such as the British and the Russians, are already, or are going 'metric', because the metric system is simpler. When Europe is the dominant economic bloc, the euro will be a key international reserve currency, and 'metrication' will become an inexorable global process to which even the USA will have to bow.

The same applies to all those other regulatory frameworks, standards, rules and conventions, which govern economic and commercial affairs. Metrication will be part of a wider process of progressive europeanization of business, as companies, all over the world, adapt their products, services, practices and procedures to comply with the requirements of their largest market. The adoption by 324 telephone networks, in 118 countries all over the world, of the European GSM standard for digital mobile phones is an early instance of what will become a series of European victories in

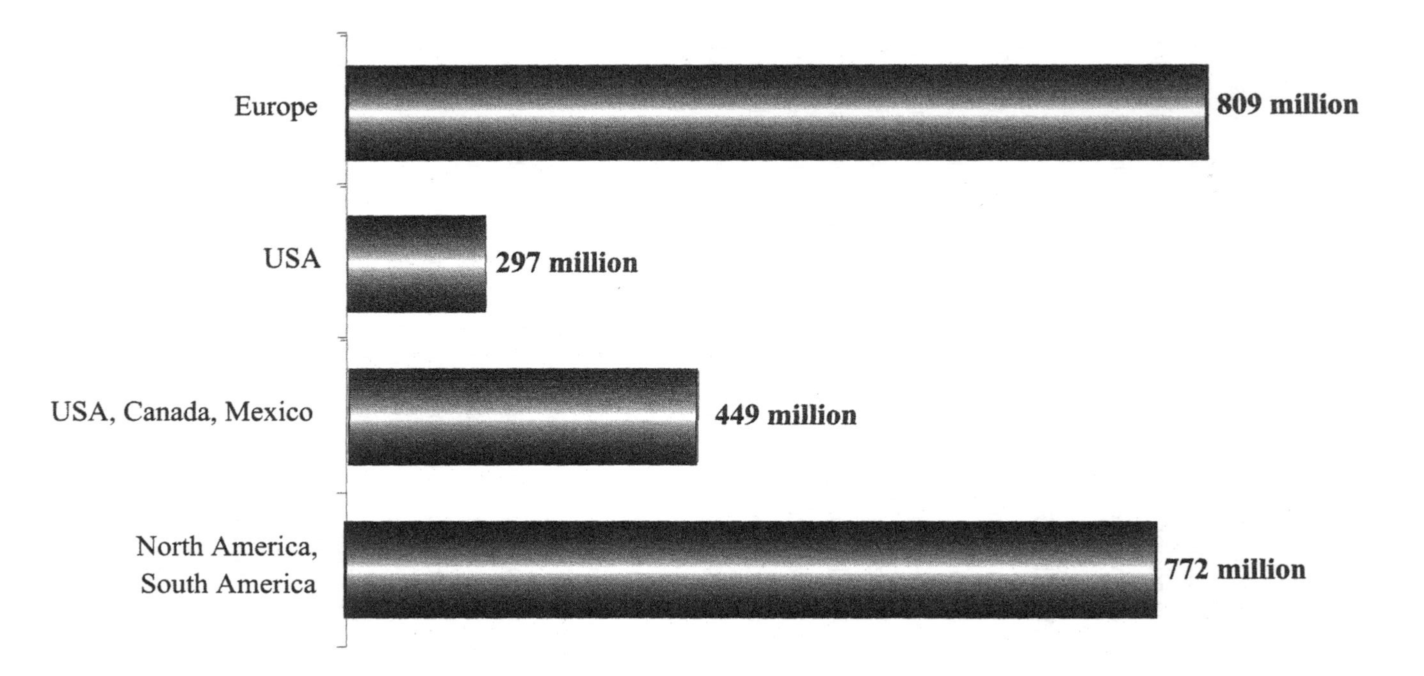

Source: International marketing and statistics 1999, Euromonitor

Figure 1.2 Population projections year 2010

technology standards battles with the USA. European standards for quality, safety, labeling, technical specifications and compatibility, design and environmental friendliness, will become world standards, not because other governments will adopt them, but because every international company will have to shape their businesses around them. For these reasons, it is vital for companies to recognize that the business world is entering a period of European economic hegemony. It may not endure much more than 20 or 30 years, but that's way beyond all but the most far-sighted corporate planning horizons. Companies that design their businesses around what they regard as Asia's inevitable rise to economic dominance will be at a serious disadvantage during the next three decades.

Why is the leadership of economic dominance now returning to Europe after its half-century sojourn on the USA? The reason is that the political developments inspired by the traumas of two devastating wars have led to a profound change in the economic nature of this previously fragmented and belligerent continent.

THE IDEA OF EUROPE

There is nothing new about the notion of Europe as a political, rather than merely a geographical unit. Julius Caesar, Charlemagne, Napoleon and Hitler were all inspired by visions of a Europe united by military conquest, and the idea of a peaceful union of European nations dates back to at least the mid-19th century. "A day will come," Victor Hugo predicted in 1849 "when you, France; you, Italy; you, England; you, Germany; all you nations of the continent, without losing your distinct qualities and glorious individuality, will merge into a higher unity and found the European brotherhood." Britain's great wartime prime minister, Winston Churchill, was a convert to the idea of a European union even before World War II. "The conception of a United States of Europe is right," he declared, in 1930. "Every step taken to that end which appeases the obsolete hatreds and vanished oppressions, which makes easier the traffic and reciprocal services of Europe, which encourages nations to lay aside their precautionary panoply, is good in itself." Churchill realized that a coming together of continental states would bring economic as well as political benefits comparable to those enjoyed by the USA.

It was not until the aftermath of World War II, however, that the intensity of national rivalry within Europe abated sufficiently to make Hugo's dream politically feasible. Once again Churchill was the leading advocate. In the first of a series of powerful speeches, the great statesman—a hero of his allies as well as of his own people—proclaimed in Zurich in 1946 the need for a partnership between France and Germany. "In this way only can France recover the moral and cultural leadership of Europe," he insisted. He added: "there can be no revival of Europe without a spiritually great Germany ... We must recreate the European family in a regional structure called, as it may be, the United States of Europe." Churchill clearly saw European political union as a way to restrain Germany. However, the French, having been invaded by Germany three times in the previous 70 years and lacking the Channel as a natural defense, felt that need even more keenly. They knew they had to think differently about security, even if it meant the loss of some of the attributes of nationhood. The idea also appealed to the guilt-stricken Germans, struggling to revive a devastated economy, both as a form of atonement and as a way to regain their status as Europeans of good standing.

It is hard to identify the precise point at which a community formed to address anxieties about security, became an economic union with a commitment to ultimate integration, but the idea of it was embedded in the Treaty of Rome, signed in January, 1958. For the business world, however, the crucial event (the point that marked the end of American economic dominance) was the birth of the euro. The enormous increase in the administrative workload during the run-up to the launch of the euro concentrated corporate minds on organizational issues. Previously, nobody had questioned the need to invoice from Milan in lire, and from Paris in francs, but suddenly it didn't make sense to be invoicing in euro from Milan, *and* Paris. And when one invoicing center emerged as the obvious arrangement for a single currency, other possibilities for major functional and process rationalizations within the euro-zone arose. When euro denominated prices, in price lists and advertisements, become the main prices, and national currency denominated prices are relegated to the parentheses previously reserved for euro-equivalents, a major psychological milestone is passed. From being an idea 'owned' by politicians and banks, EMU (European Economic and Monetary Union) becomes an everyday reality for millions of Europeans. The euro spreads like a pandemic, to stock prices, menus, labels, petrol stations, and every other price list. It replaces marks, francs, lire and pesetas as the standard measure of value in European minds and, above all, it exposes and therefore dooms, differences in real prices that were previously hidden behind national currencies.

Looking back, historians are very likely to judge the launch of the euro on January 1, 1999, as the defining moment of economic union, more significant than the Treaty of Rome itself. It is a small word, with a modest, lower-case 'e', but it has enormous implications for global business. Overnight, a pan-European market has emerged, larger than any other single currency market, and companies all over the world now have to decide whether to be part of it or to remain regional players.

ADAPTING TO A EURO-CENTRIC WORLD

In 1989, when the Berlin Wall fell and the Soviet Union collapsed, the USA emerged as the world's only military super-power. The 'American way' had vanquished all of its rivals, and the American 'business system' was free, at last, to spread throughout the world. Americans were at the top of their game and raring to go, much like the British at the end of the 19th century, when half the world owed allegiance to Queen Victoria. With their battleships in the Arabian Gulf and the sea of Japan, and their armies and aircraft on point duty in the Middle East and the Balkans, Americans could be forgiven for believing in the advent of an enduring 'pax americana'. For military power is a symbol, is it not, of economic power? How could the USA be so dominant militarily, without being equally dominant economically?

History reveals a very different relationship between economic and military power. As Paul Kennedy pointed out, military power is only a symbol of economic power, in the sense that it is a consequence of it. Nations do not become militarily powerful until they have become economically powerful and the examples of three other nuclear powers, the UK, France and Russia, show that the accoutrements of military power usually remain long after economic power has been lost. Moreover, in the modern world, the currency of military power has lost much of its value. Japan and Germany have done very well without it and Russia's example shows that attempts to build a powerful military machine on a frail and undernourished economy is a recipe for disaster. In a world from which the threat of mutual nuclear annihilation has been lifted and most security problems can be handled by relatively minor 'police' actions, the 'military superpower' is an anachronism. Once acquired, however, military power is hard to dispose of. America is likely to continue to be burdened by it, just as Britain was, long after it has lost its economic dominance. In short, great military power is becoming a liability. It is a symptom of an earlier economic dominance and, at the same time, both a presage of and a contributory factor to relative economic decline.

Americans are going to find it hard to come to terms with relative economic decline. They have become as accustomed to the dominance of their companies in the business world, as they have been to their military dominance. Until now, most of the world's largest companies have been American, because they have been nourished in the world's largest domestic market. Now that Europe is emerging as the world's largest integrated market, even larger companies are likely to emerge from the process of consolidation already beginning in a number of European industries such as defense. A landmark event in this shift of the skew in the distribution of corporate size, from America to Europe, was the acquisition by Germany's Daimler-Benz of Chrysler—the American group that makes the successors of those Willys Jeeps in which American officers orchestrated the invasion of Germany after D-Day. And BP's acquisitions of Amoco and Arco ensure that they can be run on 'European' fuel for many years to come.

America's auto industry has consolidated into three companies. If, as seems probable, economic integration leads to a comparable consolidation of the European auto industry, the companies that emerge from it are likely to be significantly larger than the American trio. For various reasons, such as the pattern of shareholdings, state ownership, restricted voting rights and different currencies, in the past M&A (Mergers and Acquisitions) activity in Europe had been slow to gather pace. By creating a pan-continental stage for corporate strategists, however, the single currency has stimulated consolidation, and European companies, in industries such as oil, pharmaceuticals, chemicals, financial services and defense, are merging, and moving up the league table of corporate size, first catching up and then overtaking their US counterparts. It seems likely that within a decade, several of the world's largest companies will be European, because Europe will be the largest market. The new breed of European super-corporations will all be global, of course, but their huge size will be a reflection of the size of their domestic market, just as the large size of America's companies today has been the consequence of the size of their domestic market. European super-corporations will want to form or buy US businesses, because the American market will still be very important. However, it will cease to be the only crucial market, the market in which all companies wishing to be global will have to be strong.

That market will be Europe, and that is 'The European Challenge'.

2
The New European Zoo

Until recently, multinational companies had only operated in western Europe, and most of them had chosen to organize their operations around the large European economies—Britain, France, Germany, Italy and in some cases, Spain. The other smaller countries were typically reporting to the European CEO, through a 'VP-small markets'. It was just about manageable having five or six senior executives 'running the geography' in Europe and reporting directly to the CEO. Greater Europe presents a much more formidable organizational challenge. Its 44 nation states range, in population, from Andorra's 100,000 to Russia's 149 million. The population of Greater Moscow alone is some 10 million—roughly the size of Portugal's. Per capita income, at purchasing power parity (PPP) rates, ranges from under €1,500 in Romania, to over €40,000 in Luxembourg, and the variations in labor costs are equally wide. Moreover, most of the ex-Soviet economies are growing faster than their new western trading partners, some at rates similar to those achieved by the Asian tiger economies in the early 1990s. That old 'a direct report for each large economy' approach to running the European geography, will not work, now that there are 25 important European countries and the 10 most important in terms of population are all larger than The Netherlands (see Figure 2.1). Organizational charts will have to be re-drawn, because it is clearly impractical to have over a dozen direct reports running the European geography.

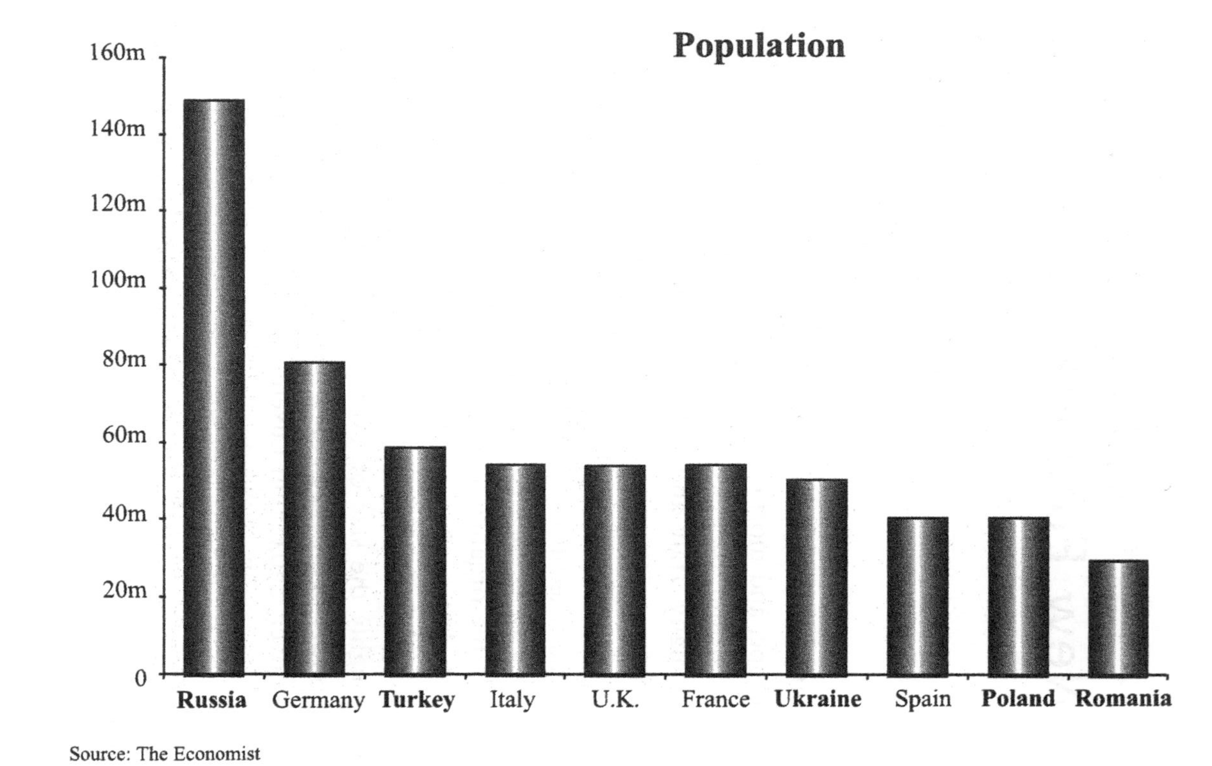

Source: The Economist

Figure 2.1 Top ten countries in population

Some may argue that the opening up of eastern Europe poses no significant organizational problems for companies, because it has come at a time when the geography-based organization is being replaced by the business-based organization. It is true the business-based organization is becoming more common, but that does not mean the 'geography' goes away. On the contrary, finding ways to run the geography more efficiently is an essential part of the shift to a business-based organization, because overheads have to be allocated over a smaller business base. A common adaptation of the old system, which embraces the ex-eastern bloc countries, without unduly increasing the number of direct reports, is to create an 'eastern Europe' division. It seems sensible. It is simple, and there's a lot to be said for simplicity. Since ex-Soviet dominated countries share a lot of history, it seems logical to bundle them together.

The trouble with this solution is that organizational changes need to be durable, because each change disrupts formal and informal communication channels within the company and so reduces productivity. It follows therefore that the fewer the design changes, the better, and designs that do not anticipate the future are unlikely to be durable. It is true that the former eastern bloc countries share a lot of history, but they strongly resented the Russian domination and always maintained their own distinct identities. Now they are free of the Soviet hegemony, they're integrating with the western European and world economies at very different rates and rapidly becoming more distinct from one another. They can no longer be treated as a 'bloc'. Each eastern European country has to be considered on its own merits.

GIVING DUE WEIGHT

One way to approach the organizational challenge posed by the expansion of Europe is to set priorities by ranking countries according to their size and the degree of their 'integration' with the world economy, one indication of which is the direct foreign investment they have attracted. Figure 2.2 shows inflows of direct foreign investment in 1997 and the stock of foreign investment accumulated up to 1997, for major recipient countries. Taking such investment as an indicator of integration, one can construct a diagram showing the most interesting markets.

Another key variable, when prioritizing markets, is the speed of de-regulation, not just in countries, but also in industry sectors. This helps to produce a clear, customized picture of market potentials and suggests the appropriate priorities for pursuing them. Figure 2.3 summarizes the opportunities, before adjustment for specific industry sectors. The top right quadrant includes countries it is imperative to be in, now. Countries in the bottom right quadrant should be planned for with a degree of urgency that depends on the de-regulation trajectory they are on. Today Russia, Turkey, Poland, the Czech Republic, Hungary and Romania emerge as the six top opportunities for international companies. Take Poland, for example. The country is de-regulating as fast as possible in anticipation of EU entry and food laws already largely conform to EU requirements. For most consumer goods sectors, it's already quite late in the day for new entrants. Competition is forcing prices down and increasing advertising costs, making market entry more and more costly. Soon after SC Johnson Wax entered the market in 1990, it noted that TV advertising costs were doubling, in dollar terms, every six months, while the number of competitive brands was burgeoning.

Russia is still significantly more regulated than Poland, but is de-regulating fast. It is roughly where Poland was about five years ago, so companies should be planning for entry, as a matter of urgency. The domestic production of many consumer goods collapsed after the fall of the Berlin Wall and imports soared. In the early 1990s, demand for western toiletries and cosmetics was growing at 10% a year. Since then, the devaluation of the ruble, a revival of local production driven by improved quality, the growing 'buy Russian' sentiment and the increasingly rigorous imposition of import duties,

	1997 $ million	Stock $ billion
Poland	5,600	20.6
Hungary	2,300	17.0
Russia	2,800	9.3
Czech	1,300	8.2
Romania	1,200	3.8
Slovenia	300	1.9
Bulgaria	1,000	1.8
Ukraine	530	1.7
Slovakia	300	1.2

Source: EBRD

Figure 2.2 Foreign direct investment (1997)

have made life harder for importers. Recently, the US Department of Commerce reported that: "The size of the Russian [cosmetics and toiletries] market is enormous, but the days of quick and easy profit have already passed."

Everyone knows that standards of living vary enormously among greater Europe's new members, and are far lower than those in western European economies. However, there are good reasons to doubt the usefulness of the usual measure of GNP per capita as an indicator of a country's importance as a market opportunity. The first is the obvious one: it is population size and total GNP that matters, not GNP per head. The Swiss are very rich, but for most multinational companies, Switzerland ranks as a minor business development opportunity because of its small population. The second reason why organizational architects would do well to be wary of per capita GNP is that, although populations do not change dramatically over time, the degrees of integration and the levels of GNP do. Organizational architects must look to the future, and recognize that the potential of a market is determined, not by how rich its people are today, but how rich its natural resources and levels of education are likely to make them tomorrow.

Official figures show per capita income is growing rapidly in eastern Europe. Euromonitor predicts that between 1995 and 2005 the core economies of eastern Europe, including Russia, Poland, Hungary and the Czech Republic, will have grown on average at least three times as fast as the core economies of western Europe (Germany, France, Italy and the UK). Over time, Figure 2.3 positions on the horizontal axis are unlikely to change much, but all the countries will move up the vertical axis at different speeds, as they become progressively more integrated with the rest of the global economy. Today, Russia appears to be an economic basket case lurching from one crisis to the next, but it is destined to become one of the world's most important markets. Although its official GNP per capita is less than a tenth of Germany's (about €2,200 a year), Russia is very rich in natural

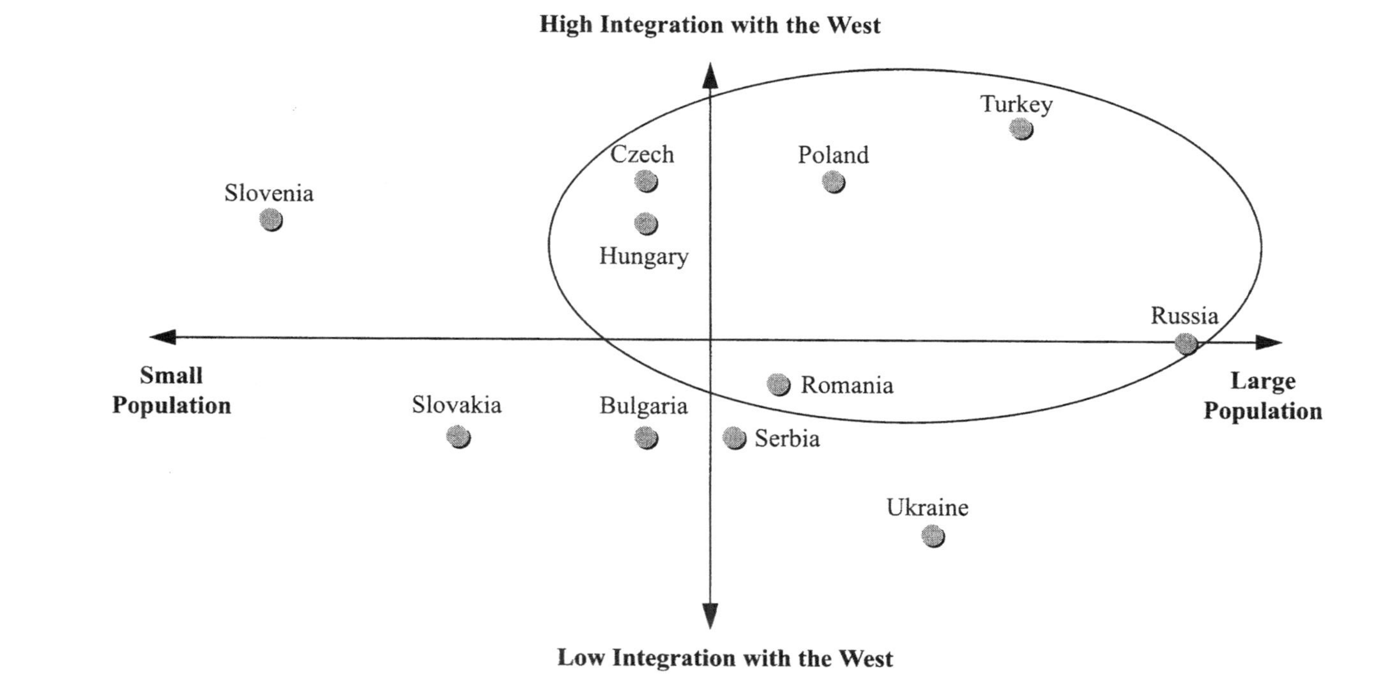

Figure 2.3 Priority setting

resources, and its 150 million people are better educated in vital subjects, such as science and math, than Americans. The third reason why GNP per capita is a poor guide for those designing organizations, is that the official statistics are wildly inaccurate, as those who have recently visited Russia, and seen the scores of Mercedes-Benzes and BMWs cruising the streets of Moscow, will tell you. Actual purchasing power in most eastern European countries is far higher than the official data indicate, because the official data cannot monitor the 'black' economy, estimated to account for between 25% and 50% of total income.

The diagram can help multinational companies give appropriate weights to greater Europe's new entrants when designing their organizations, but it leaves open the question of how the new geography should be managed. Companies also need to find some way to handle the greater complexity of the enlarged European economy.

CLUSTER MANAGEMENT

The best way to reduce complexity to a manageable level is to group clusters of markets around a few key countries, because neighboring economies inevitably develop links that lead to closer integration. As already noted, in the old days the UK, France, Germany, Italy and sometimes Spain, were usually seen as the natural focal points from which to manage Europe.

Questions arise about which minor countries should be managed from which focal points. Switzerland, for example, being trilingual, could be managed from France, Italy, or Germany. The fact that 80% of the Swiss watch German television, however, suggests that the solution that maximizes business synergies is to have Switzerland report to Germany. Similar questions arise about Belgium, but the choice is more clear cut with Austria, which is obviously within the German sphere of influence. Proximity and cultural similarities make a strong case for managing Greece from Italy.

But what of the new entrants? If it is inappropriate to group them together into a single eastern Europe cluster, as argued above, to which focal point should Poland report for example? The obvious answer is to declare Russia, the most interesting of the new greater European markets, a new focal point and to manage Poland from there. But this merely creates an 'eastern European' cluster in another way, and takes no account of the widening of the differences between Poland and Russia, on the one hand, and the narrowing of the differences between Poland and its western neighbors on the other. The rate of Poland's economic integration with western Europe (as indicated by foreign investment and the fact that it is among the 'first wave' of new EU members) is significantly higher than Russia's. It's true that, for historical reasons, the Poles do not like the Germans any more than they like the Russians, but they much prefer to see themselves as a part of the richer, more stable German sphere of influence. This shift in orientation is reflected in the trade flows. In 1997 over a third of Polish exports went to Germany whereas Russia—once Poland's primary trading partner—only absorbed 8% of its exports, and almost one quarter of Poland's total imports came from Germany while only 6% came from Russia. If Poland is linked with Germany, to what focal points should Turkey, the Czech Republic, Hungary or Romania be associated? What criteria should be used, when assembling the 'clusters' of greater Europe? Designers of new organizational structures could be forgiven for breaking a few pencils, wearing their erasers out, and wishing in their frustration that Europe was more like North America.

THE AMERICAN MODEL

Europeans tend to look at North America (and particularly the USA) as a highly homogeneous market, with only minor regional variations. It is true North America consists of only three major countries, Canada, the USA and Mexico, and that it has been unified by railways, airlines, radio and television for more than a century, but it is very far from being the homogeneous market it is usually seen

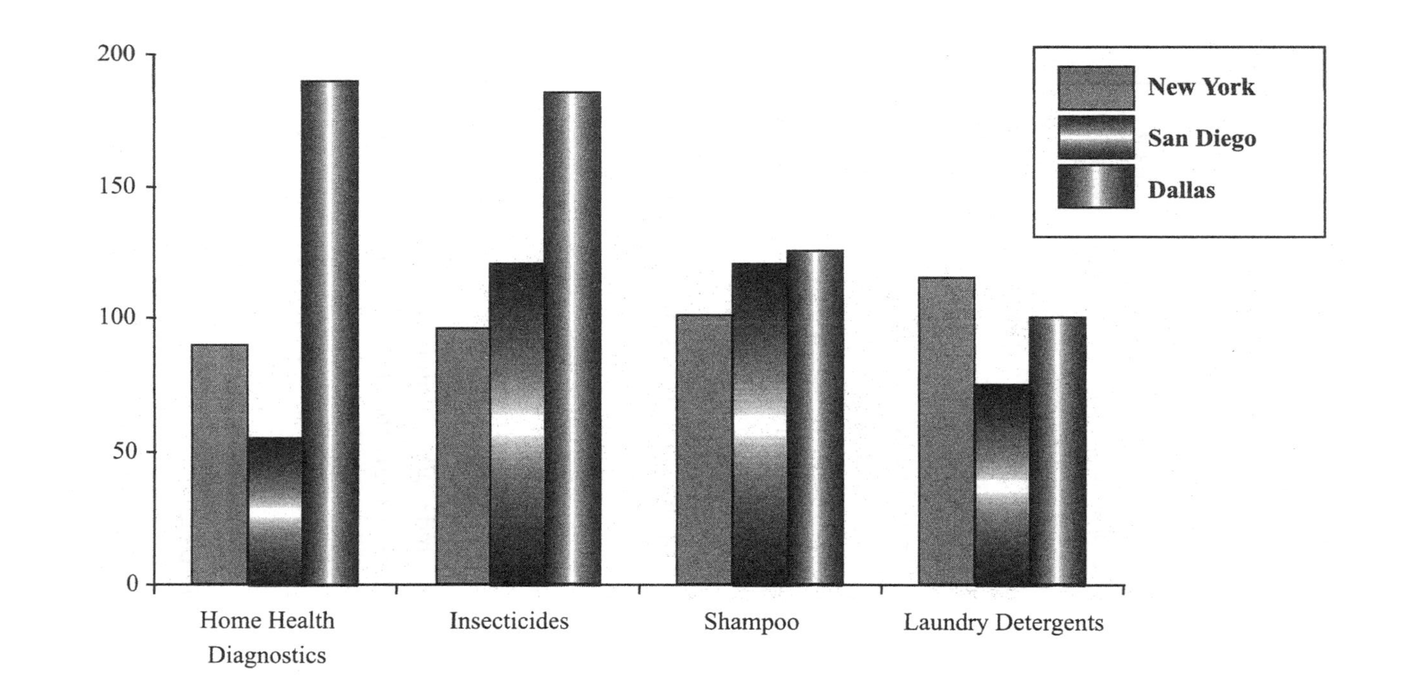

** Average per capita consumption = 100*

Figure 2.4 Per capita US Consumption Index 1997*

to be. Consider Figure 2.4. It shows indices of per capita consumption for four household product categories in three US cities—New York, San Diego (California) and Dallas (Texas). The differences are substantial and some are quite puzzling. One would expect the insecticide consumption to be lower in New York than Dallas and San Diego, because there tend to be fewer mosquitoes and flies in higher latitudes, but why the big difference between Dallas and San Diego, which are on roughly the same latitude? And why do the citizens of Dallas buy four times as much home health diagnostics as the citizens of San Diego?

In the early 1980s, before NAFTA was created, journalist and social demographer, Joel Garreau, caused quite a stir by suggesting that North America should be seen as consisting, not of three, but of nine nations, whose borders do not appear on any map. His book, *The Nine Nations of North America* was based on his travels through North America and his realization that the stamps on his passport gave no hint of the very different countries he had visited. Figure 2.5 shows Garreau's map of North America.

In the north-east there is Quebec, a small Francophone, Roman Catholic island surrounded by water and Anglo-Saxons. It is rich in cheap 'hydro' electricity (and the industries, such as aluminum smelting, attracted by it). Men love big cars, women are 'chic', cooking is an art, labels on packaging must be in two languages and bilingual managers are *de rigueur*. To the south-east of Quebec is New England, birthplace of the USA, and strongly Anglo-Saxon. According to Garreau, it takes in Labrador, Newfoundland, Maine, Vermont and New Hampshire, and stretches down to Boston. As the oldest of the nations, it was the first to lose its early power and influence, but has since exploited its prodigious intellectual assets, to become a favored location for new, high technology industries. Travelling south-west brings one to The Foundry; the industrial heartland around the Great Lakes, bordered by Wisconsin in the west, and taking in the lakeside cities of Chicago, Detroit, Cleveland and Toronto, as well as Pittsburgh, Baltimore and Philadelphia to

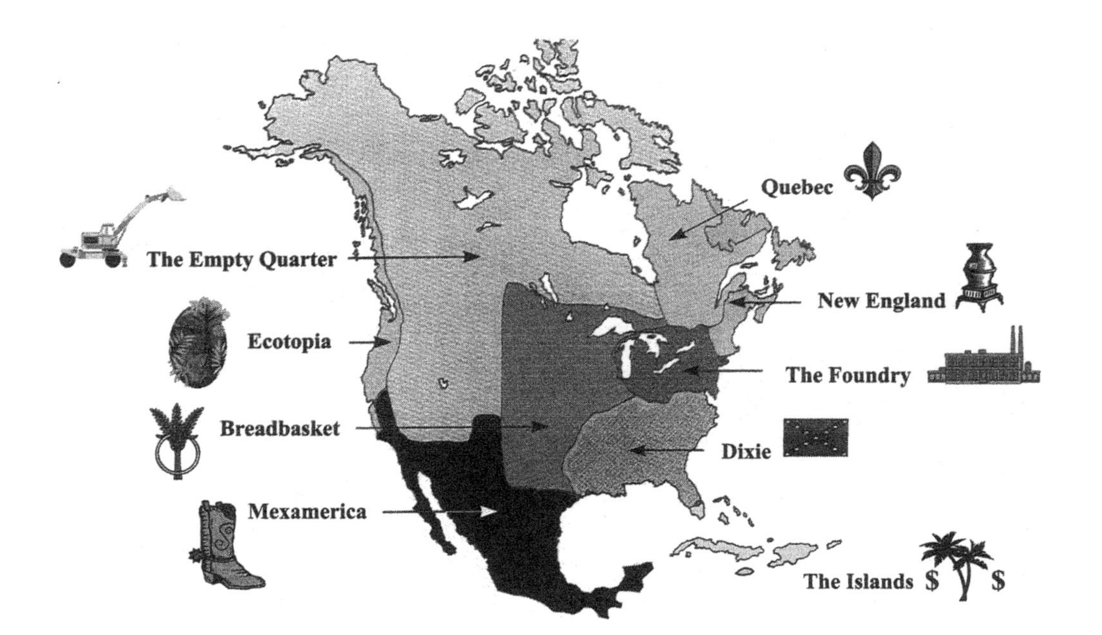

Figure 2.5 Although North America has been a common market for more than 100 years, it is still divided into nine major clusters

Map from *The Nine Nations of North America*, © 1981 by Joel Garreau. Reprinted by permission of Houghton Mifflin Company.

the south. Blessed with plenty of water, minerals and people, it was the natural crucible for America's industrial revolution. It has been in decline since, because its industries have taken the brunt of European and Asian competition, but has shown some signs of a revival since Garreau's book was published.

South of The Foundry is Dixie, bordered by Chesapeake Bay and the Ohio and Mississippi rivers. The Allegheny Mountains are its backbone, and Atlanta, Richmond, Memphis and New Orleans are its major cities. Dixie is more of an idea than a region, and, although regarded as the backward 'south' by Yankees, it has been growing rapidly, and is rich in oil, cotton, tobacco and music. South-east of Dixie are The Islands, including Miami, all the Caribbean islands and the Colombian and Venezuelan coasts. It provides tax shelters for the rich, and sun, sand and sailing for holidaymakers, and retired people. Miami is a port of entry for drug dealers, and the city that has long been most favored by multinational companies, for their Latin American headquarters. The Breadbasket, as its name implies, is the continent's main granary. It accounts for around 75% of North America's grain and much of its cattle and pig meat production, and is a major wheat exporter. It stretches from Saskatchewan and Manitoba, in Canada where, as Garreau noted, 'carbohydrates become more important than hydrocarbons', down to the Gulf of Mexico. Its industrial capital is Kansas City, its cultural and business capital is Minneapolis, and as befits a predominantly farming area, its politics and general outlook are conservative. Most of its people are of northern European extraction and consume vast quantities of fast food and barbecue fare.

North and west of the Breadbasket is the Empty Quarter, a huge, mountainous area rich in coal, oil, alumina, uranium, iron ore, steel mills, churches and ski resorts, but 'dry' in both senses of the word—water is scarce and the consumption of liquor is frowned upon by the churches. It incorporates almost all of Alaska, most of western and central Canada, all the Rockies, and reaches down to

Denver and Las Vegas. South of the Empty Quarter is Mexamerica, stretching from the Sierra Nevada in the north, to the Sierra Madre in the south, and including Los Angeles, Mexico, New Mexico and Arizona. It has a distinctly Hispanic culture, and at the time of writing Garreau was predicting that it would soon replace The Foundry as the continent's dominant and most populous nation. Finally, there is Ecotopia: a thin stretch of fertile land to the west of the coastal mountain ranges, that stretches from Anchorage in the north, and runs southwards, through British Columbia to Seattle, Portland, San Francisco and San Jose. It is a wet region, flanked by the Pacific and constantly washed by fresh water from the vast mountain ranges to the east. Its people feel psychologically, as well as geologically isolated from their neighbors to the east and south, and share a deep love of, and concern for the environment.

It was not Garreau's purpose to provide a model for corporate organization in North America, but the distinctive economies, climates and cultures of his 'Nine Nations' have implications for business. The lines that divide them suggest the patterns of consumption in North America are affected by unchanging or slowly changing factors: proximity to natural geographical barriers such as rivers and mountain ranges, climate, income levels, demographics and whether people live in cities or the countryside, in houses or apartments. People don't settle within nations. They settle in particular places and, over generations, they impart to, and acquire from their places distinctive appetites, accomplishments, and attitudes to life and work, that together create distinctive regional cultures and personalities. It's the clustering of these qualities, not state or national borders, that shapes North America's markets, and there is no reason to suppose Europe will be any different.

THE CLUSTERS OF EUROPE

The same variables that have divided North America into 'Nine Nations', population, income, demographics, types of housing, climate, and proximity to, and separation by natural barriers from other nations, are carving out the same kind of clusters on the other side of the Atlantic. Language, cultural and national identities and traditions, and the historical relationships between them, are playing a more important role in shaping the clusters of greater Europe, but in the decade since the Iron Curtain opened, they have ceased to divide the continent in two. The old battle line is just one of a number of cluster-shaping factors at work within the context of a strong trend towards economic integration. So what are these clusters and how can they be characterized?

The first step in defining greater Europe's emerging clusters is to identify the continent's centers of economic gravity. Figure 2.6 shows Europe's nine largest countries by population, and their respective shares of total European GNP in 1995. This generates Figure 2.7, showing that greater Europe's dominant countries are Germany, France, the UK, Russia and Italy. These are the focal points, around which the smaller countries are likely to cluster. Taking all the cluster-shaping factors into account, produces a map of greater Europe consisting of four main clusters (see Figure 2.8)

We will explore the natures of the clusters in more detail in the next four chapters, but let us name them here and describe some of their principal characteristics.

- The Northern Bees—*Germany, The Netherlands, Scandinavia, Poland, Hungary, the Czech Republic, Slovakia, the Baltic States, Austria and Switzerland*
  This is an industrious and methodical 'cluster', whose people enjoy already, or aspire to, high per capita incomes. Germany is obviously dominant, but the cluster includes several major non-German cities and centers of activity and its eastern flank is being integrated very rapidly. It specializes in manufacturing, its workers are generally highly organized and its labor markets are relatively rigid. Its cultures are based on strong social values, and its peoples have become increasingly ecologically sensitive.

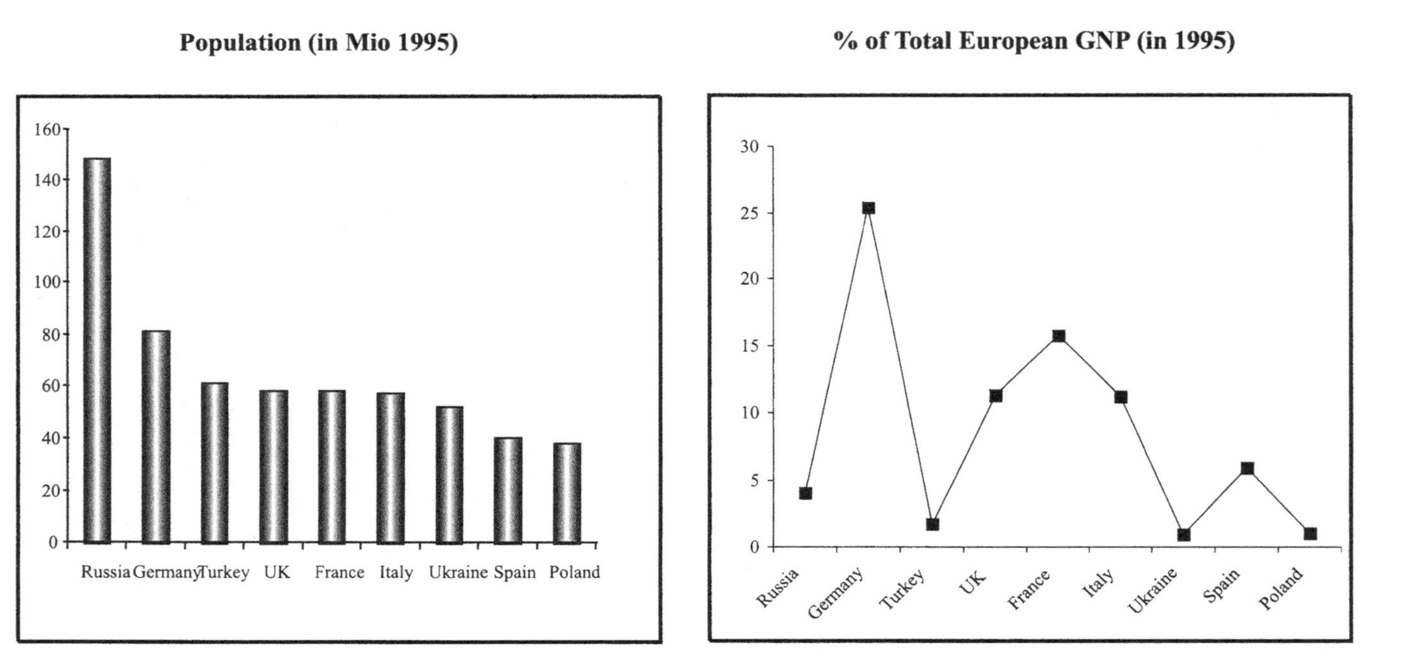

Figure 2.6 The economic importance of a country is not only determined by its population size, but also by its market share of European GDP

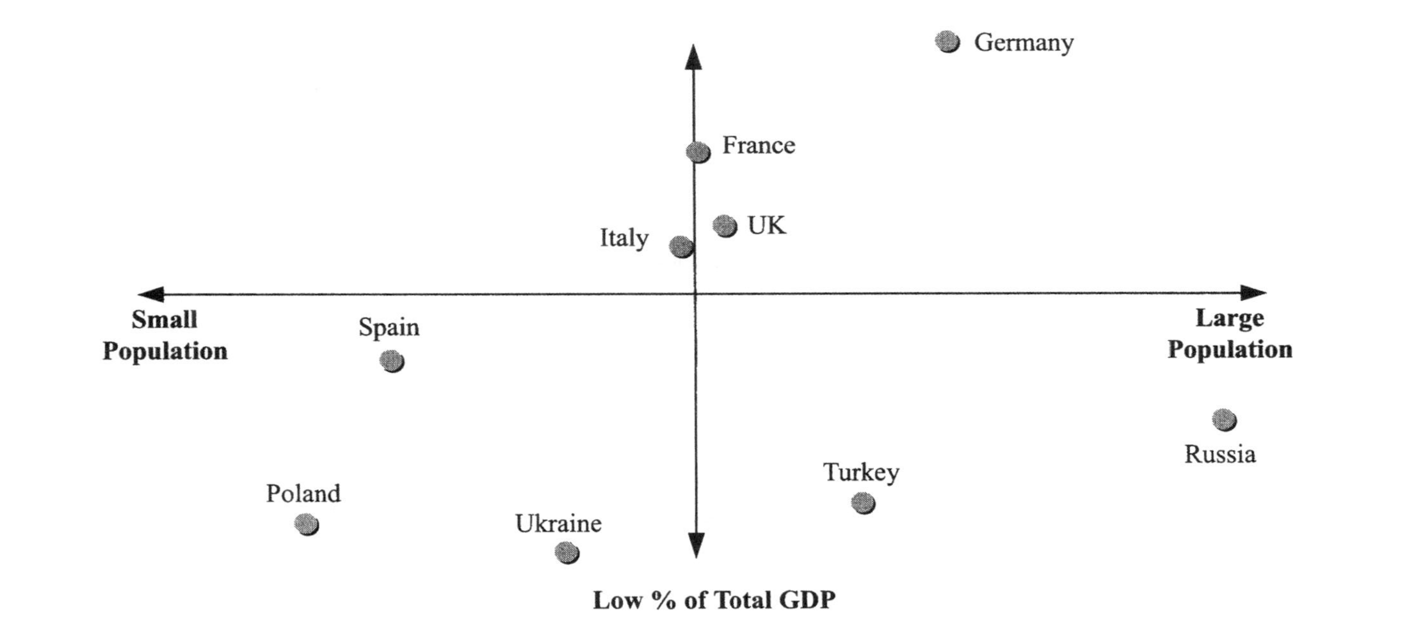

Figure 2.7 Combining both population and GDP, the most dominant countries in greater Europe are Germany, France, UK, Russia and Italy

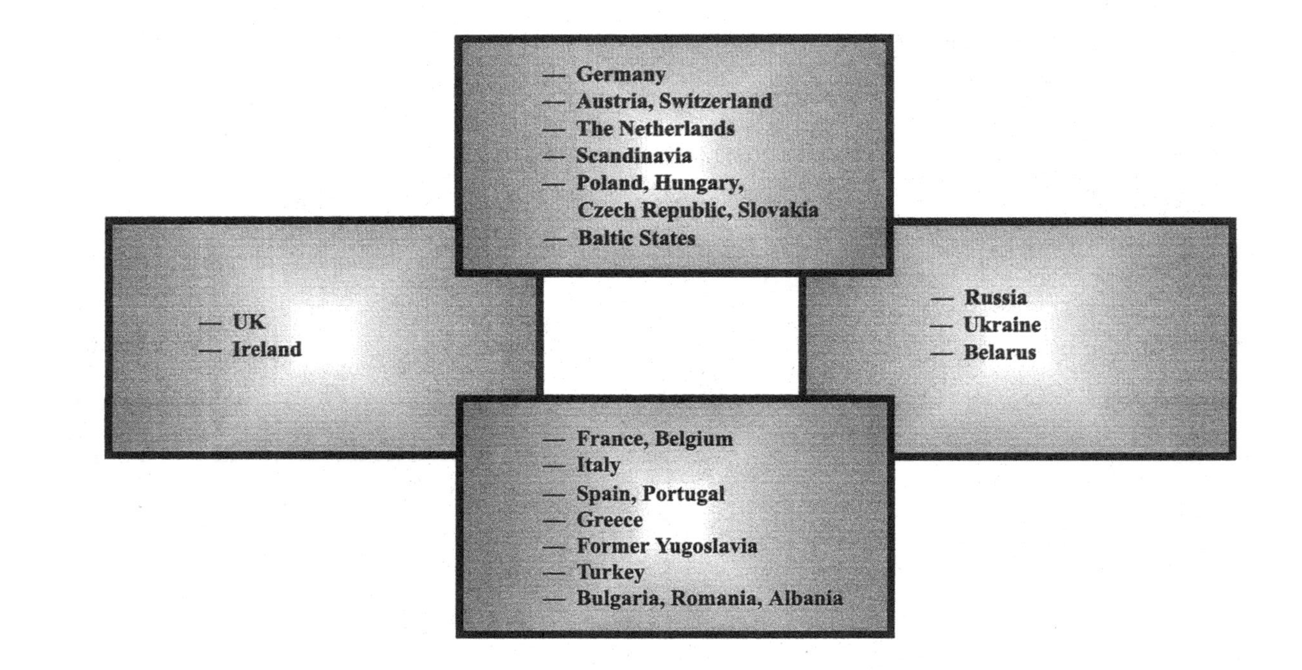

Figure 2.8 Based on population, GDP and proximity, four key European clusters could be identified

- The Atlantic Storks—*the UK and Ireland*
  Pulled equally towards Europe and the USA (for which it often acts as a bearer of new ideas), this small, two-nation cluster is independent, pragmatic, and physically and psychologically insular. Its economy is increasingly service-orientated, and its labor markets are significantly more flexible than those of continental Europe. Ireland has been the economic success story of this cluster in recent years, but the UK will always be the dominant economy.

- The Southern Gazelles—*France, Belgium, Italy, Spain, Portugal, Greece, the Balkan countries, Turkey, Bulgaria and Romania*
  This is a multicentric cluster with no dominant country. Its people are individualistic and entrepreneurial, and gazelle-like in their flexibility and constantly changing priorities. Although its working methods are not as organized as those of the Northern Bees, the importance of ideology in its members' societies have caused its labor markets to become similarly rigid. Other distinctive characteristics of this cluster are the relatively large proportion of total GNP accounted for by tourism, and the slow rate at which the cluster's new eastern flank is being integrated.

- The Eastern Bears—*Russia, Ukraine and Belarus*
  This three-nation cluster of countries is dominated by Russia and remains nationalistic, inward looking, and suspicious of the West. Its government and institutions are unstable, but it is very rich in natural resources and has a highly skilled and low-cost workforce.

COMING TOGETHER AND APART

One advantage greater Europe has over North America is a single currency. For the time being, the independently minded British are not participating in European economic and monetary union. However, when the bulk of greater European business is conducted in euros, and internal financial flows are not subject to the same distortions as those caused in North America by the periodic weaknesses of the Mexican and Canadian currencies. Cultural integration is also proceeding apace. A decade or so ago, it was easy to tell European nationals apart by the sorts of clothes they wore. Nowadays, everyone wears blue jeans and Benetton shirts and English is rapidly emerging as the common language of Europe (and of the world). The emergence of English as the lingua franca of Europe is a development of enormous economic significance, because it facilitates communications and eliminates subtle psychological barriers to the movement of people and the exchange of ideas.

English is emerging as Europe's language, not because, or not just because, it is the language of the USA, the largest market in the world (pro tem), but also because it is much simpler than the other languages in use in Europe. Latin languages decline verbs, Germanic languages decline adjectives, Slavic languages decline both, but English declines neither. Because English is not a phonetic language, spelling is difficult, but automatic spell-checkers are now standard on all computers, a lot of business communication is verbal (telephone or videoconference), and command of the intricacies of English spelling is unnecessary, when absorbing the language through music, radio, cinema and television.

The Canning School in London—a leading ESL (English as a Second Language) college for business people—reports that, over the past ten years, enrolment from the Southern Gazelles has fallen, because more English is being taught in their local schools. Enrolment for courses in advanced presentational skills has risen dramatically, however (particularly by Northern Bees students), and attendance by eastern European students has tripled over the past five years. It will take a long time for the local languages to degenerate into dialects, but Europe's polyglot heritage has its silver lining: Europeans feel much more comfortable in foreign countries than Americans, and are better at adapting their thinking and actions to the cultural differences that still enrich the world. Although the lack of 'pension portability' has so far restricted the number of Europeans who live permanently in European countries in which they were not born to less than 10% of the total, Europeans travel a lot more within Europe and are beginning to feel more comfortable in each other's countries. As Figure 2.9 shows, the number of foreign residents in each country there has grown dramatically over the past decade.

But at the same time as Europeans begin to feel more European they are beginning to feel less ardently national. The Scots, Welsh and Basques demand independence, Slovakia has separated peacefully from the Czech Republic, and there is secessionist pressure in northern Italy. Nationalism is still strong in former eastern bloc countries, but throughout most of Europe the old, national allegiances are being gradually replaced by regional affiliations. In 1992, just after the signing of the Maastricht treaty that created the euro, Dr. A.H. Heineken, argued that Europe was too large to be run as a single country and, because country borders did not properly reflect the cultural affinities, he proposed that Europe be divided into 75 districts, each with a population of five to ten million. It would be like America, whose people introduce themselves by saying: "I'm an American, from Boston (or Philadelphia)," not "an American, from Massachusetts (or Pennsylvania)." It seems likely that, before long, Europeans will introduce themselves by saying: "I'm a European, from Paris (or Milan)."

The emerging feeling of European identity is least evident in the UK, but despite the failure of successive UK governments to take an unequivocal stand on Europe, opinion polls suggest that the number of Britons who want to withdraw from the EU has been falling steadily over many years. Whether they are willing to admit it or not, most Britons are beginning to feel less emotional about their national identity. This is because the process of economic integration is driven, not by treaties and formal policies, but by the changes in popular attitudes created by increased levels of cultural

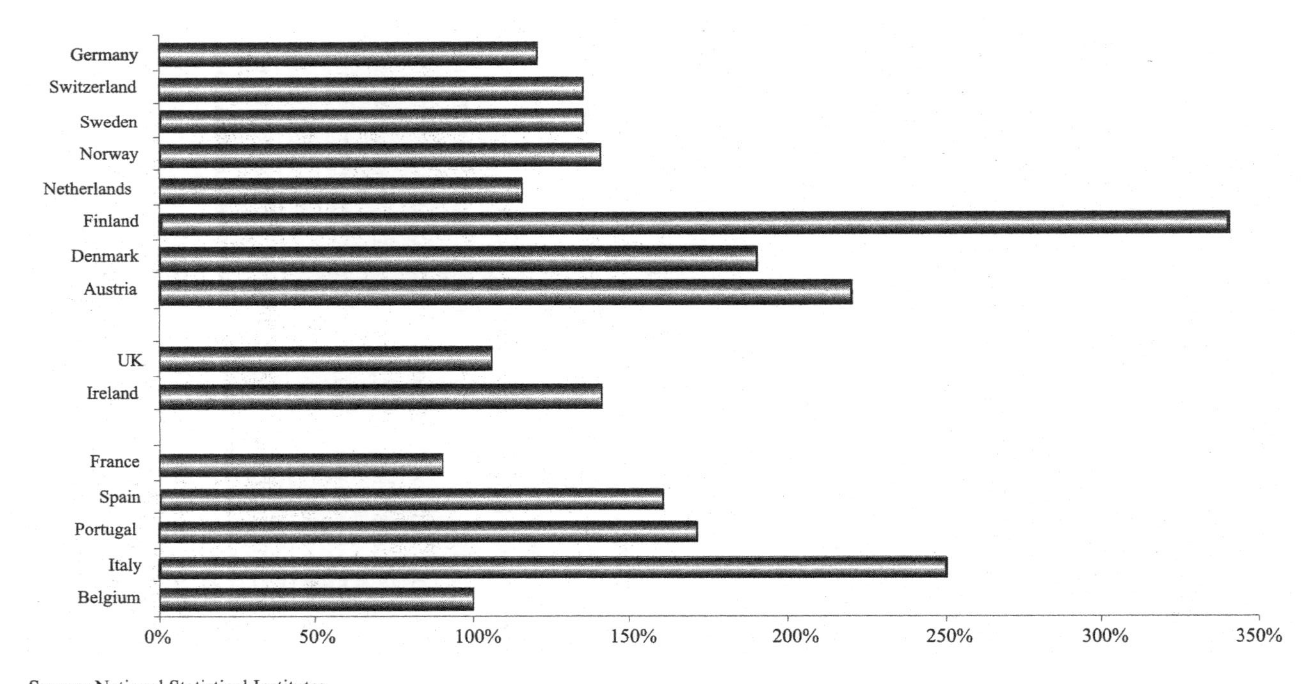

Source: National Statistical Institutes

Figure 2.9 Growth in foreign population – 1986 to 1996

and economic interaction and the gradual emergence of a common outlook. The UK is likely to be the last western European country to integrate fully with Europe, but because English is the European lingua franca, it's unlikely to become isolated in the way Quebec is becoming isolated from the rest of North America.

It is clear that organizational designs that fail to take into account the disintegrative, as well as the integrative forces at work in the current re-configuration of greater Europe are unlikely to stand the test of time. The idea that markets are always coming together in some ways and coming apart in other ways is already commonplace in North America. Large companies are integrating their manufacturing operations, supply chains and increasingly their marketing throughout Canada, the USA and Mexico and undertaking a lot of local promotional initiatives at the same time. It is equally clear that new organizational designs for Europe that do not employ some kind of variety reduction model, will be hard, if not impossible to manage. In the next four chapters, we will look in more detail at the zoological four-cluster model of Europe introduced above, and put the case for regarding it as a powerful variety-reduction model for business managers, that is unlikely to be overtaken by foreseeable events.

Europe is now, and will remain, for many years, in a state of considerable economic and cultural flux, but its bees, bears, gazelles and storks are distinct and well-established species that are unlikely to change their habitats, and their ways of life overnight.

3

The Northern Bees—Germany, Austria, Switzerland, The Netherlands, Scandinavia, Poland, Hungary, the Czech Republic, Slovakia, and the Baltic States

The Northern Bees cluster is not the most populous of greater Europe's four clusters, but it is by far the most productive. Its total GNP is €3.8 trillion, compared to €3.7 trillion for the Southern Gazelles cluster, which is home to almost 50% more people (see Figure 3.1).

A distinguishing feature of this cluster is its dominance, in terms of both output and population, by one country. Germany is Europe's industrial powerhouse and its population is more than twice as big as the cluster's next most populous country, Poland. Moreover, German political power will increase, as its large population gives it more representatives than any other European country in European institutions. It was the political might of a re-united German population, not the economic might of Germany's industries, that caused such concern elsewhere in Europe, and particularly in France, at the time of re-unification. Whether or not other Europeans find the idea palatable, there is no conceivable development in the foreseeable future that can prevent Germany

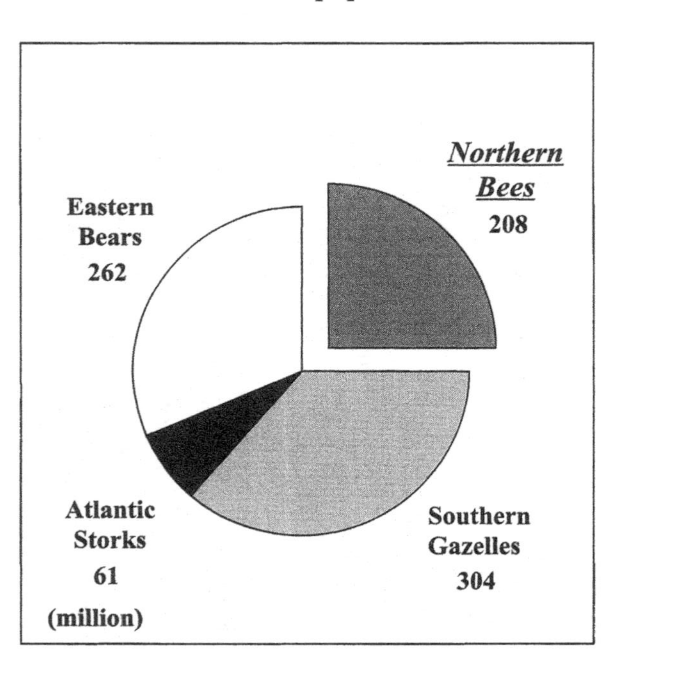

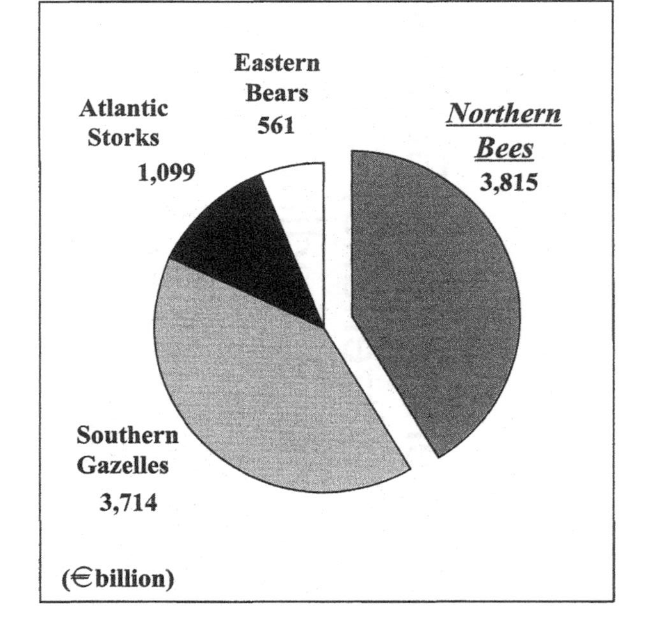

Source: The Economist Pocket World in Figures 1999

Figure 3.1 Clusters' population and GDP

and the cluster of neighboring countries whose political and economic destinies are linked to it, from becoming Europe's dominant cluster. If anything, the integration of the cluster's eastern flank is likely to accelerate the process, because for the strong business reasons discussed below, it's happening more quickly than the integration of the southern ex-Soviet countries.

DIMENSIONS OF INTEGRATION

The forces that are welding the Northern Bees cluster into a culturally and economically coherent area are many and varied and interact in subtle and complex ways, but the facts about trade, investment and communications, leave no room for doubt about the momentum behind the process. Trade is a powerful instrument of both cultural and economic integration, because with each exchange of goods or services, there is an exchange of attitudes and outlooks, the cumulative effect of which is very significant. Those who trade with each other, gradually come to resemble each other, and the Northern Bees have in the past, and are continuing to trade with each other more than with other European countries and clusters. Germany has always had strong trade links with its neighbors in western Europe, and in recent years its trade with eastern European and Scandinavian countries has been increasing at an accelerating rate (see Figure 3.2).

During the period 1989–96, Germany's trade flows (exports plus imports) with Poland, the Czech Republic and Slovakia almost quadrupled, and its trade with Hungary more than trebled during the period. These growth rates were considerably higher than the rates of growth in the trade of these four countries with France, the UK and Russia, with the exception of France's trade with the Czech Republic and Slovakia which grew rapidly, from a very low base in 1989. As a result, Germany is today by far the most important trading partner for all these key eastern European countries (see Figure 3.3). Investment flows in recent years also add to the picture of a new, enlarged cluster. In 1995, eastern Europe's

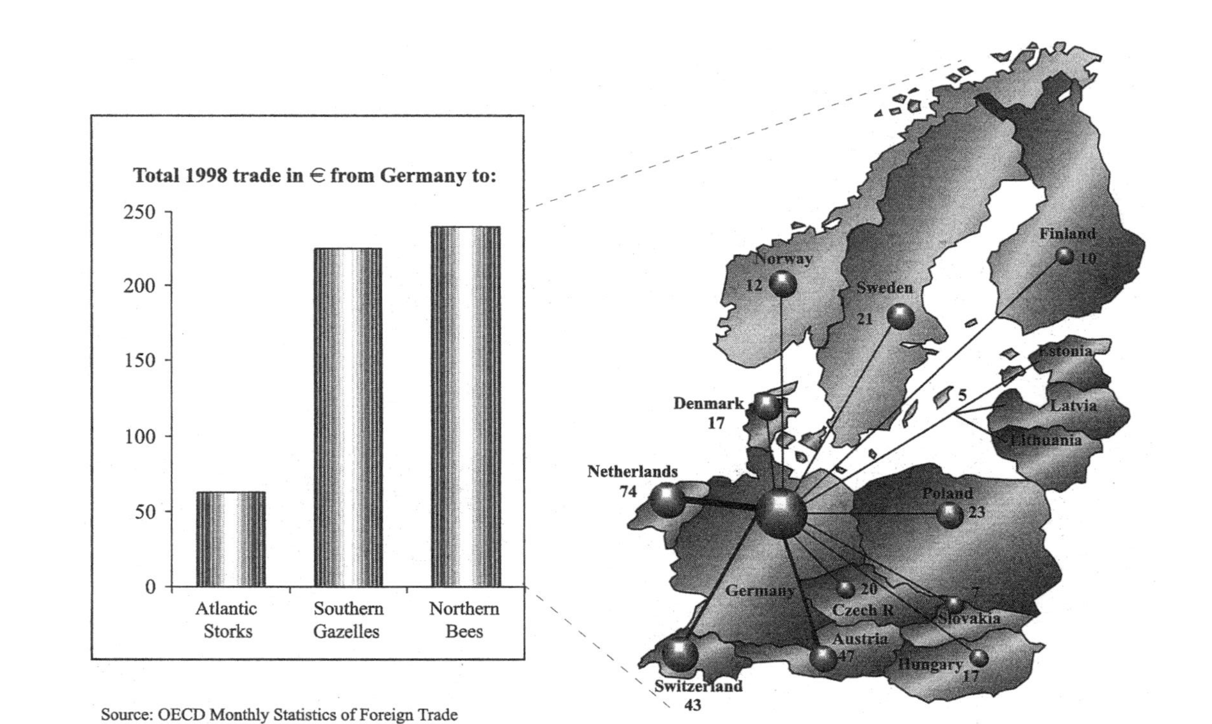

Figure 3.2 Germany trades not only heavily with its German speaking neighbors, but increasingly with eastern Europe and Scandinavian countries

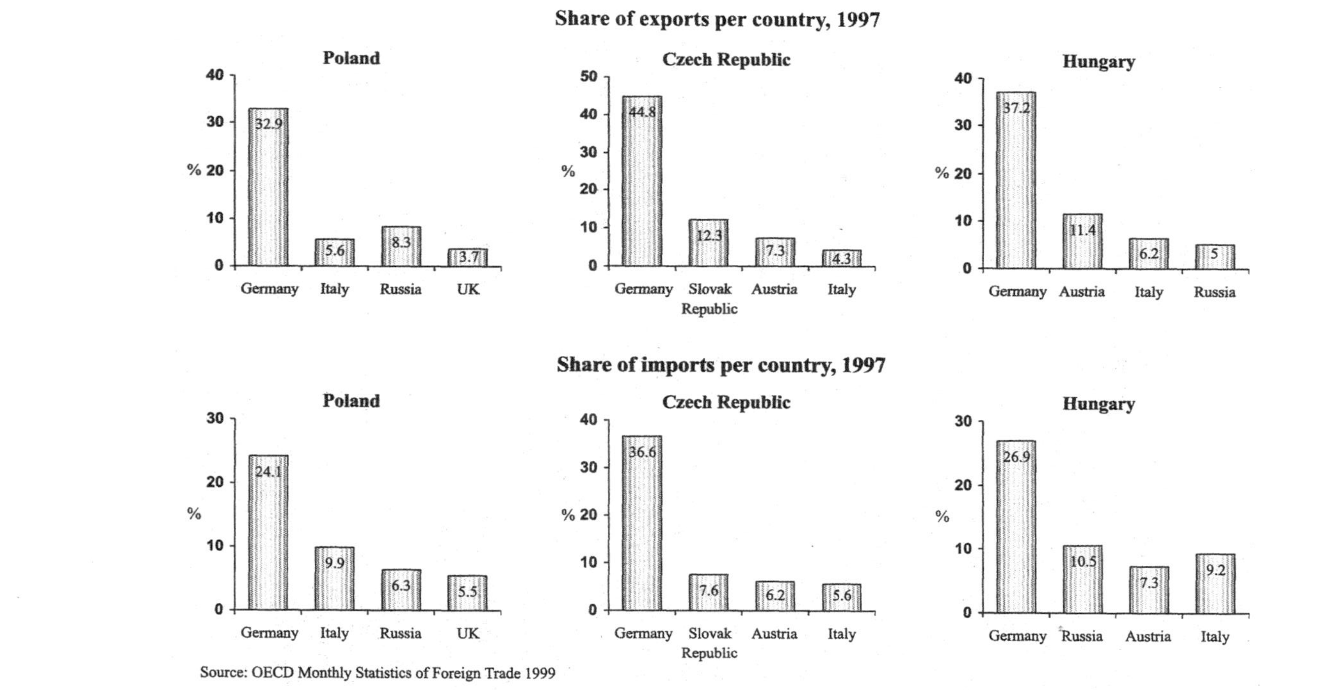

Figure 3.3 Germany is the most important trading partner of Poland, the Czech Republic and Hungary

Northern Bees' countries—Poland, Hungary, the Czech Republic, Slovakia and the Baltic States—accounted for over half of Germany's foreign direct investment (FDI) in Europe. Moreover, A.T. Kearney's FDI Confidence Index, derived from the investment plans of major multinationals, shows that investment in Poland is due to increase substantially over the next few years.

The reason for the interest of German industrial investors in their country's eastern neighbors is simple. They saw there an answer to their prayers: the chance to escape the pressure on their competitiveness exerted by their strong currency—before the Deutsche Mark (DM), and now the euro—and their high and ever rising labor costs. The opening up of the Iron Curtain has given German firms an opportunity to construct major extensions to their manufacturing systems in neighboring countries that possess two invaluable, rarely combined qualities—high levels of education and low salaries. The acquisition of Skoda by Germany's Volkswagen Audi Group (VAG) demonstrates how this eastward expansion of manufacturing capacity allows German companies to shift their domestic activities to higher value-added areas. Skoda cars, once the butt of western jokes ('the Skoda is a 16-valve car: eight valves in the engine and eight in the radio'), are now so good that they came top of the 1998 and the 1999 J.D. Power/Top Gear UK surveys of buyer satisfaction, ahead of BMW, Mercedes and the Japanese brands. Skoda is now a VAG 'transplant'—a manufacturer of re-badged Volkswagens, designed and engineered in Germany. The transplant would not have worked as well nor as quickly in India or Nigeria, because those countries lack the required education levels in their workforces, but the Czech Republic (with its German-like work ethics) is an ideal transplant territory.

This is the great strength of the Northern Bees cluster. There is a 'symbiosis' between its strong western flank, struggling with the problems of economic success and its newly liberated eastern flank, able and eager to provide the solutions. The symbiosis is made all the more fruitful by the importance of industry among Northern Bees.

Industry accounts for 37% of Northern Bees' gross domestic product (GDP), compared to 31% for the Southern Gazelles. Of Europe's top seven 'industrial countries', five are Bees (see Figure 3.4). The attachment of the industry-orientated neighboring states will help ensure that the Northern Bees cluster retains its position as greater Europe's industrial heartland.

Trends in travel patterns tell a similar story of progressive cluster homogenization. The three diagrams on Figure 3.5 show the number of non-stop flights from western Europe's six main airports in Germany, France and the UK, to the capitals of the Czech Republic, Poland and Hungary. German people, as well as German trade and money, are increasing the attachment of these recently freed neighbors to the Northern Bees cluster.

Northern Bees are also talking with each other more and more (see Figure 3.6). Although the Swiss and the Dutch are Germany's largest correspondents for out-going telecommunications, traffic between Germany and Hungary, Poland and the Czech Republic has grown rapidly.

Language also binds Northern Bees together. All of them, with the exception of the Baltic States, which speak Russian, have strong German-speaking traditions. The linguistic affinity is reflected in the preference of television viewers in these states for German-language TV channels (see Figure 3.7). Thus, in addition to the process of economic integration revealed by the statistics, a process of cultural osmosis is under way, that is causing the peoples of the Northern Bees cluster to become more like each other in their outlooks, and their general behavior. They are becoming culturally as well as economically coherent.

VALUES AND ATTITUDES

What kind of people are these busy, industrious Bees that are giving a new coherence to northern Europe? How do they think, how do they live and work, and what values do they hold dear? More to the point for business people, are they sufficiently different from their

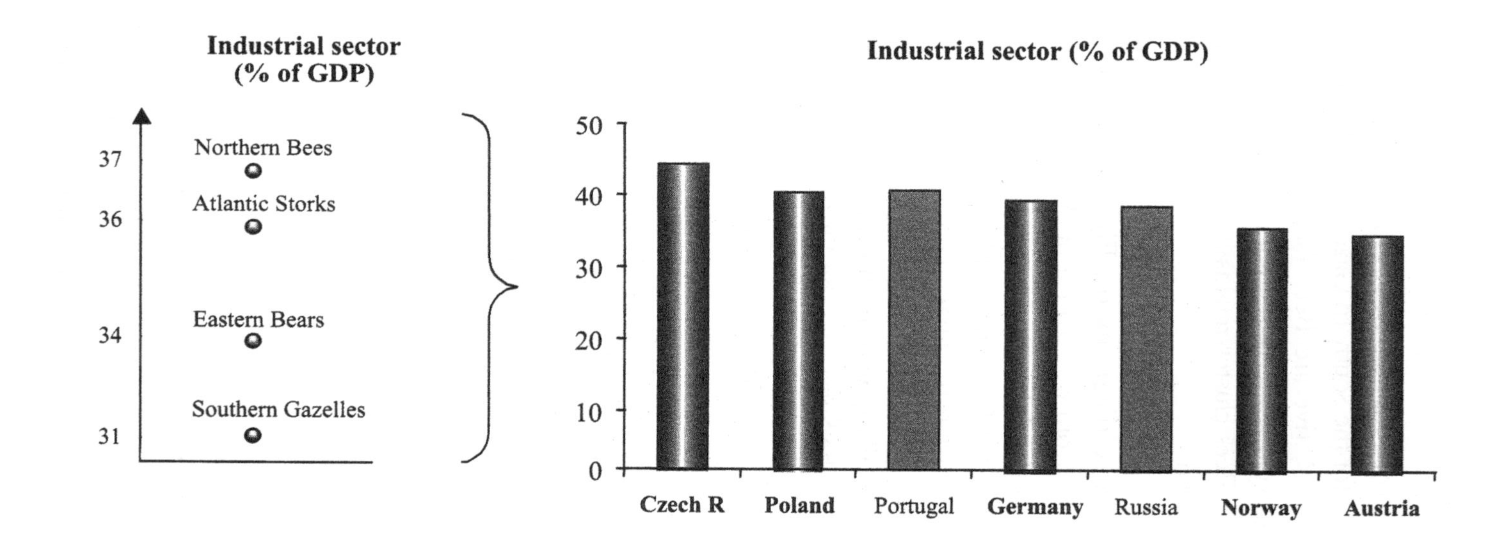

Source: World Competitiveness Yearbook 1997

Figure 3.4 The countries of the Northern bees are focusing on industrial production. Five of the top seven industrial European countries are part of this cluster

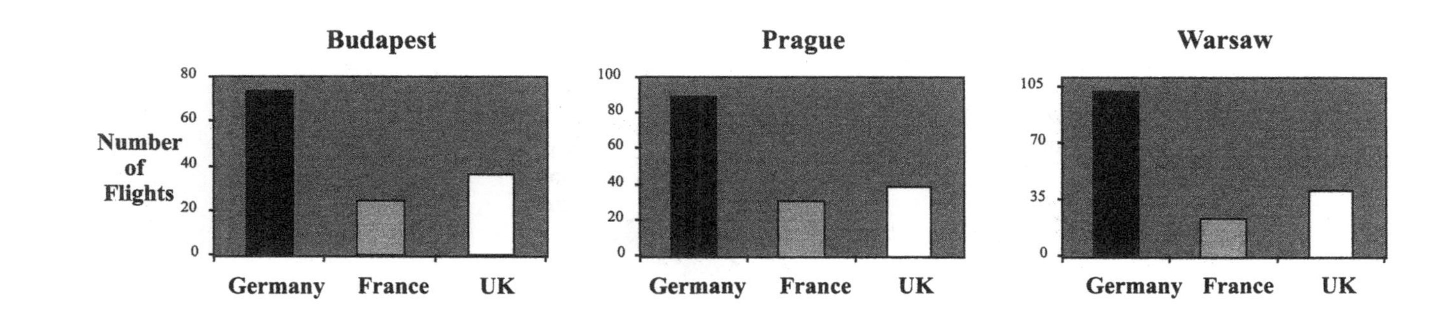

Number of non-stop flights from the six main airports to Prague, Warsaw and Budapest as of September 1998

Figure 3.5 From all clusters' main cities, Germany have by far the most flights to Budapest, Prague and Warsaw

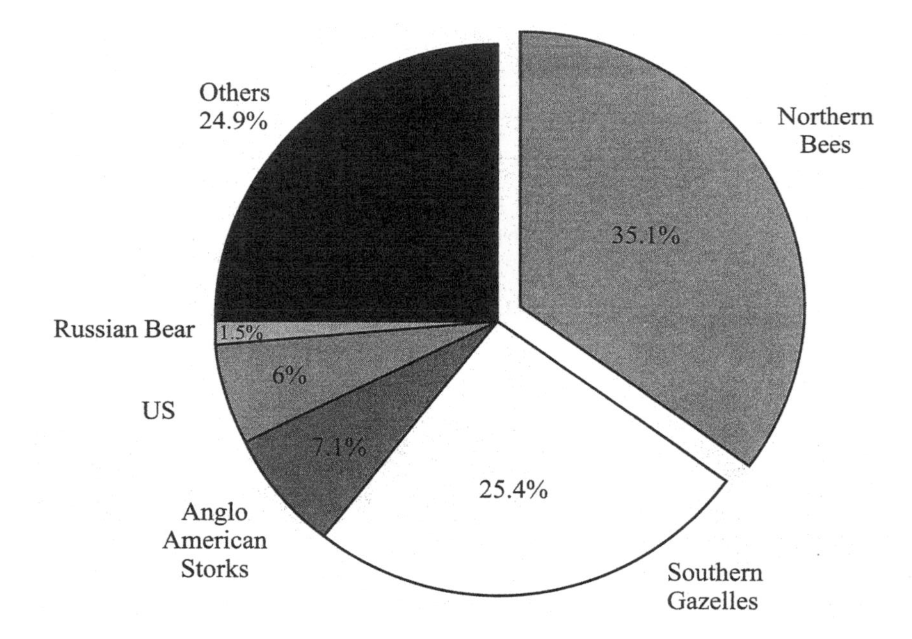

Traffic flows in MiTT: Minutes of Telecomunications Traffic in mio of minutes of public switched traffic
Source: Telegraphy, 1977

Figure 3.6 Northern Bee's Telecommunications traffic

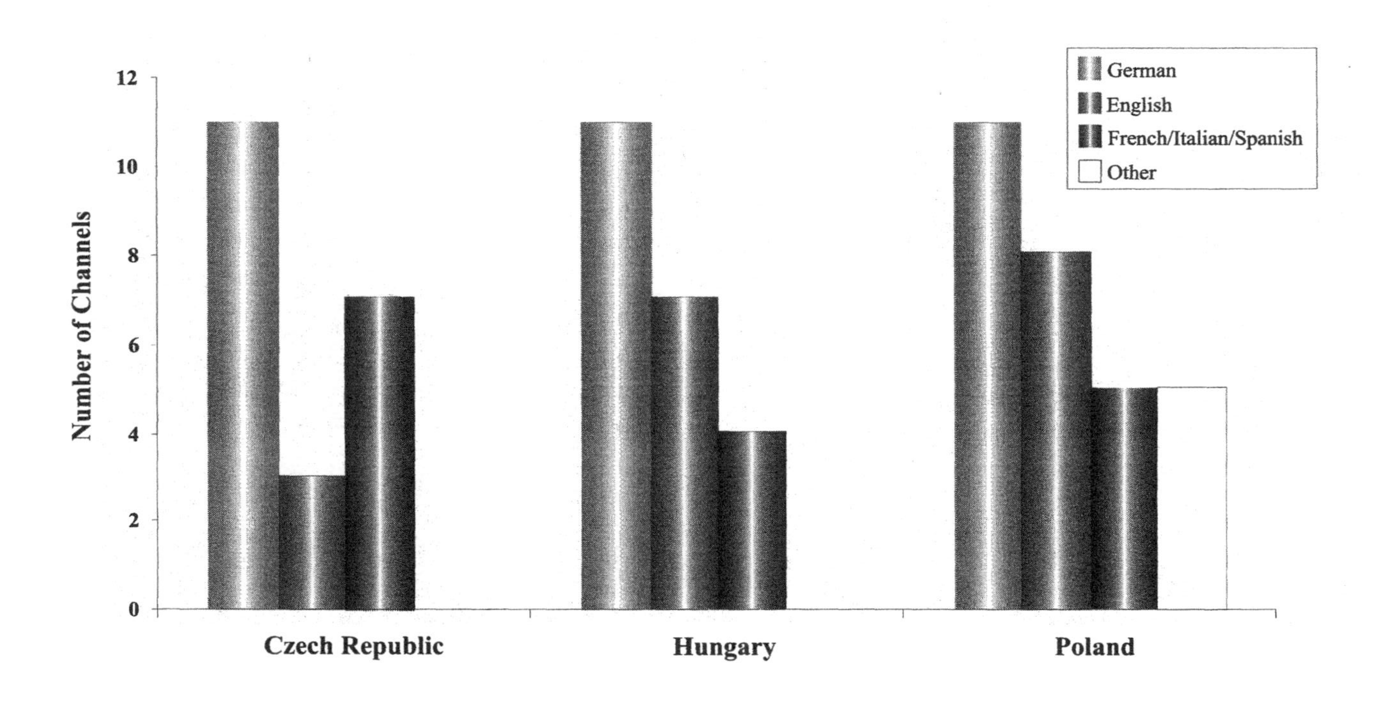

Source: Television 97

Figure 3.7 German is by far the dominant language among all foreign and pan-European channels viewed

neighboring countries to the east, west and south, to represent a distinct market? This first point to note is that although the Northern Bees are dominated by Germany, Germany itself is not dominated, to the same extent as other European countries, by one major city. A strong, federal tradition has survived in Germany, since its original unification by Prussia in the 19th century, and this has led to an unusual (by European standards at any rate) de-centralization of economic and political power. Berlin has become a huge construction site in recent years, as business flocks to the former (and new) capital, in the belief that it is ideally placed to become northern Europe's major city. However, the size of Frankfurt, Düsseldorf, Hamburg and Munich as well as that of other important cities, such as Stockholm, Copenhagen, Amsterdam and Rotterdam in the west, and Warsaw, Prague and Budapest in the east, gives the Northern Bees cluster some of the character of a federation of city states rather than nations.

The federal character of German government is also evident in German business organization, where the 'Konzern' (a group of associated businesses, often including banks that still hold large equity stakes in German industry) is a characteristic form, rather reminiscent of the Japanese keiretsu. Similar business federations also exists in Scandinavia, Switzerland and The Netherlands where very large multinationals dominate the economy. The coherence of the cluster is sustained, not by a monolithic economic and cultural center, but by a set of characteristic values and attitudes, the origins of which are debatable, but probably owe much to climate, geography and history. The Scandinavians, for example, lead the cluster in the emancipation of women. According to the 1998 Human Development Report of the UNDP, there are more women in Parliament in Scandinavia than in other European countries, and, for that matter, in the USA and Japan (see Figure 3.8). This trend is extending to Germany and even to conservative Switzerland, where women only won the right to vote after a 1971 national referendum.

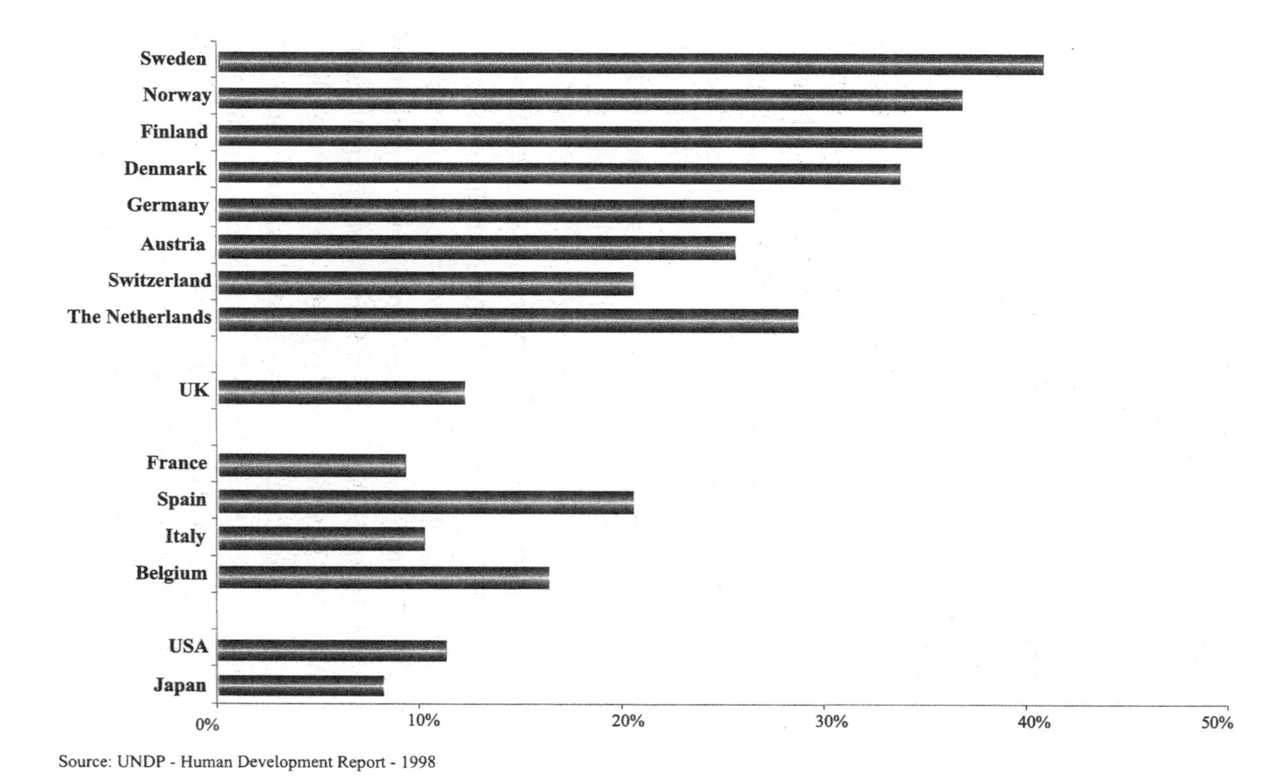

Figure 3.8 Seats in parliament held by women

The Northern Bees are, by and large, very law-abiding. They obey the rules, and prize order in their homes and communities. Swiss city streets are quiet at night, compared to those of France, Spain and Italy; public places in Holland and Scandinavia are clean, and well-kept; and in western Poland, where the German influence is strongest, cars tend to be parked tidily. But, as Lech Walesa in Poland and Germany's Green politicians have shown, the taste for order and balance is not associated with an unquestioning respect for authority. Germany's Greens have attracted strong political support with their confrontational approach to ecological reform, and their outspoken disgust at the way German industry had poisoned the Rhine. In recent years, their political success has led to a raft of strong environmental legislation in Germany. The French and Italians would look in disbelief at anyone who suggested that people should be fined for washing their cars in the street, but such laws have been enacted and are generally observed in Germany. This is because Germans know and care about what detergents can do to the flora and fauna of community sewage systems.

Germans are wealthy, but careful spenders and see added value in goods and processes with a low 'environmental impact'. The Rhine has been cleaned up, but the trauma of its post-war poisoning has left an indelible mark on the German psyche. A number of explanations have been offered for the remarkable strength of the green movement in Germany (mirrored elsewhere in the cluster, particularly in Scandinavia, Switzerland, Austria and The Netherlands where ecological labeling of goods is now ubiquitous). Some say it is because Germany has a very short coastline, relative to its size, and this has obliged it to absorb more of its industrial waste on land. Others say that strong green movements always emerge in rich, heavily industrialized countries, where pollution is a constant problem, and ordinary people are rich enough to be able to afford the higher costs of their ecological purchases. Whatever the reason for it, the ecological sensitivity of the Northern Bees makes them excellent markets for environmentally friendly goods of all kinds. Indeed it seems fair to say that the Northern Bees cluster is the only cluster where ecological awareness has a significant impact on consumer behavior. It is no accident that the German group, Bosch, led the world in the development of green (low water consumption) dishwashers and washing machines.

Another deep trauma has been caused by the hyperinflation of the 1920s and of the late 1940s. No other western European country has encountered so little popular resistance to the low inflation policy, and none have pursued it so long. Policed single-mindedly by an independent central bank, the low inflation policy caused the DM to become the world's strongest currency, and exerted a powerful influence on setting up the mandate of the European Central Bank in its management of euro interest rates. It has also led to the failure of innumerable German companies and, compounded by high wages and high non-wage payroll costs, it has caused unemployment to rise to uncomfortable levels in recent years. Yet no one questions the need for it. German industrialists may have complained about the DM's strength, but they would not dream of voting for a party that was not committed to maintaining price stability. And they insisted that the euro should be at least as strong as the DM.

Inflation is a persistent German nightmare for another reason too: it makes it hard to plan. The importance of industry to the German economy, particularly price-driven industries such as car making and chemicals, makes the long planning horizons permitted by stable prices highly desirable. But there's more to it than that. Germans, like the other Northern Bees, are organized and methodical, to the core. That's why they are such good manufacturers. They don't work particularly hard—vacations are long, and the working day is strictly 9 to 5—but they are far more organized than other European societies. They don't waste time and effort on trial and error. They get things right first time. Some have suggested that this German passion for organization and the methodical approach, makes it unsurprising that SAP, the world's fastest growing computer software company and the pioneer and dominant supplier of enterprise resource planning (ERP) systems, is a German company. When Thomas H. Davenport wrote in the *Harvard Business Review* (July–August, 1998) that 'the reason enterprise systems first emerged in Europe is that European companies tend to have more rigid, centralized organizational structures than their US counterparts', he had in mind SAP in particular and German companies in general. It is not Europe as a whole that is unusually organized, but its Northern Bees cluster.

Germans admire qualities like reliability and durability, and set far more store by competence ('kompetenz' in German) than other Europeans. In English, people are merely competent, and by implication, lacking in creativity. To attribute 'kompetenz' to people in German, however, is to praise them very highly. The respect for 'kompetenz' dates back to the 19th century, when Germans, in their efforts to catch up with England in industrialization, developed networks of trade schools (Gewerbeschulen) to produce technical middle managers, and technical high schools (technische Hochschulen) to produce generations of chemists and engineers. Today over 70% of German employees are technically qualified, compared to only 30% in the UK. This German 'ethos' was well summarized by a Frenchman, Paul Valéry, who, 100 years ago noted: "Germany owes its success to a concept hated by certain cultures—especially the English and French cultures. This concept is discipline. It should not be overlooked. It in fact possesses another name: intellectually speaking, it is called method, ... A Frenchman or an Englishman can invent a method. They have already proved it. They can also submit themselves to a discipline; and they proved this too. But, they will always prefer something else. For them, it is a 'least worst solution', a temporary solution, or even a sacrifice. For a German, it is life itself."

The methodical, organized German approach is very appropriate for manufacturing, but is much less valuable in fast-changing businesses such as fashion, where flexibility is at a premium and companies in the Southern Gazelles cluster, like Benetton, excel. It is similarly unsurprising, therefore, that the only impact German companies have had on the fashion industry has been in the less mercurial men's fashion business. And even the best known German fashion 'griffe', Hugo Boss, has been acquired by the Italian textile group Marzotto. The lack of flexibility (also evident in German unions, which share the distaste of employers for short planning horizons) is, according to some observers, just as deeply rooted in the German psyche as the desire for order and organization. It is evident, for example, in the strict timekeeping at work, and the impossibility of finding a German shop open on a Sunday morning. Germans are used to such rigidities, and organize their lives and businesses around them, but some Germans see this lack of flexibility as a serious weakness in a world that is becoming less predictable by the day, and changing at an accelerating rate. They worry about a lack of innovation and are concerned that German companies are not sufficiently creative, and have been filing too few patents in recent years.

In 1993 Mercedes-Benz announced that it would be returning to single-seater motor racing after an absence of 30 years as an engine supplier. Given that excellent engineering is a source of considerable national pride in Germany, and central to the image of Mercedes-Benz itself, Germans could have be forgiven for assuming that this meant that teams of highly 'kompetent' Mercedes engineers would be designing engines for the Formula One (F1) and IndyCar championships. Not so: the only activity the Mercedes-Benz attack on F1 and IndyCar (since robbed of its Indianapolis 500 race) inspired within the giant German firm was the writing of large checks in favor of a small English firm, Ilmor Engineering. German pride in the excellence of its engineering took another blow more recently, when the original version of the much-heralded Mercedes-Benz small car, the A Class, turned over, during the so-called 'Elk test' applied by Scandinavian journalists, and 15,000 cars had to be recalled for modifications. Of course, the modified Mercedes A now has a state of-the-art electronic stabilizer that makes it much safer than its competitors.

Such signs of German fallibility apart, there can be no doubt the organized and methodical culture Germany shares with western Europe's other northern countries, and the influence it is exerting through growing economic and cultural links on the attitudes and outlooks of its new capitalist neighbors to the east, is forging a powerful and coherent cluster that is the industrial engine of Europe.

4

The Atlantic Storks—The United Kingdom and Ireland

With 62 million people the Atlantic Storks is the smallest of the four clusters, but they produce over twice as much as the Eastern Bears' 210 million people (see Figure 4.1). Their degree of industrialization, at 37% of GDP, is not much lower than that of the Northern Bees, which they resemble in others ways too. However, their language, history and culture, and the sea between them and the continent, isolate them from the rest of Europe psychologically as well as physically. England dominates the cluster to an even greater extent than Germany dominates the northern Bees. Ireland, however, is one of the EU's success stories and has become a more robust junior partner in recent years. Until a decade or so ago, Ireland was poor, and had much the same kind of relationship with its larger, more prosperous neighbor as southern Italy has with northern Italy, and eastern Germany with western Germany. After it joined the EU, however, it grew rapidly, thanks partly to large net receipts from the EU budget, which accounted for over 3% of Irish GDP at one time. Once a victim of significant net emigration, mostly to the UK and America, Ireland is now a vibrant, and prosperous society (so much so that it is no longer eligible for EU subsidies). It attracts capital and well-educated young people and is a favored location for telephone 'call centers' serving the customers of large European companies.

Historically, there has been little love lost between Ireland and the

UK. After a long and bitter struggle, Ireland won its independence in the 1920s, but had to surrender its rich northern counties, whose people, separated from the south by religious and political allegiances, clung to the 'union' with Britain. The Catholic minority in the northern provinces felt betrayed by the partition and supported the terrorist Irish Republican Army (IRA) in its campaign against what they saw as Britain's army of occupation. The Protestants retaliated with several loyalist paramilitary groups, which were just as murderous as the IRA. Thousands of innocent people died over the 20 years of 'The Troubles'. In recent years, major steps have been made towards resolving the conflict. After the landslide Labor Party victory at the 1997 British general election, Northern Ireland's 'Unionists' lost much of their political influence in Westminster, and entered the all-party talks that led in 1998 to the historic 'Good Friday' Anglo-Irish agreement. This deal required the Irish government to abandon its long-standing claim to the northern province, and obliged the IRA publicly to renounce terrorism, and put its faith in its political arm, Sinn Fein.

A similar conflict arose and was resolved in a similar way in northern Italy in the 1950s. After World War I, Italy had annexed part of southern Austria (Südtirol) and renamed it 'Alto Adige'. Mussolini felt the ethnic balance should be altered and was so successful in populating it with poor Italians from the south, that by the end of World War II there were as many Italians living in the Südtirol region, as there were Austrians. Bombs began exploding with alarming frequency, but both countries realized that the bombings would continue if the dispute was settled in favor of either of them. So they agreed to make the area bilingual, and give the region considerable autonomy. It has all bilingual road signs, a German language TV station, and German is taught in schools alongside Italian. It has been very quiet ever since, so much so that it is a favorite destination for tourists. Similarly, the solution to the Northern Ireland problem emerged from unprecedented levels of co-operation and joint policy-making between the British and the

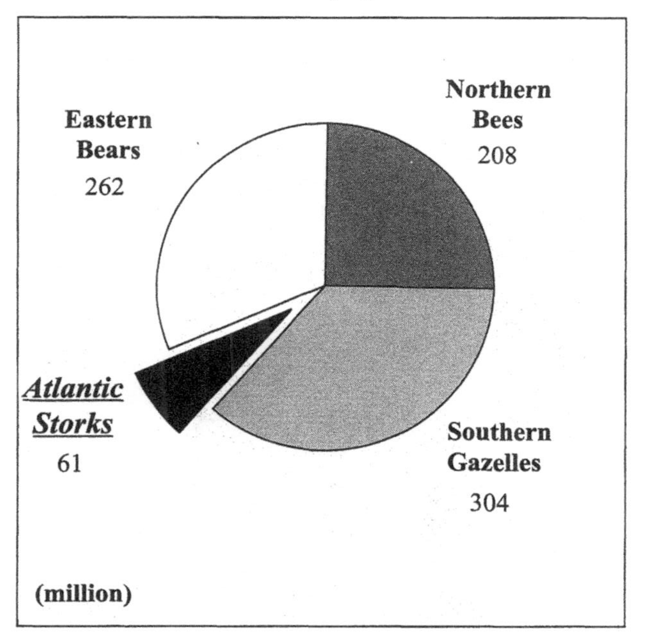

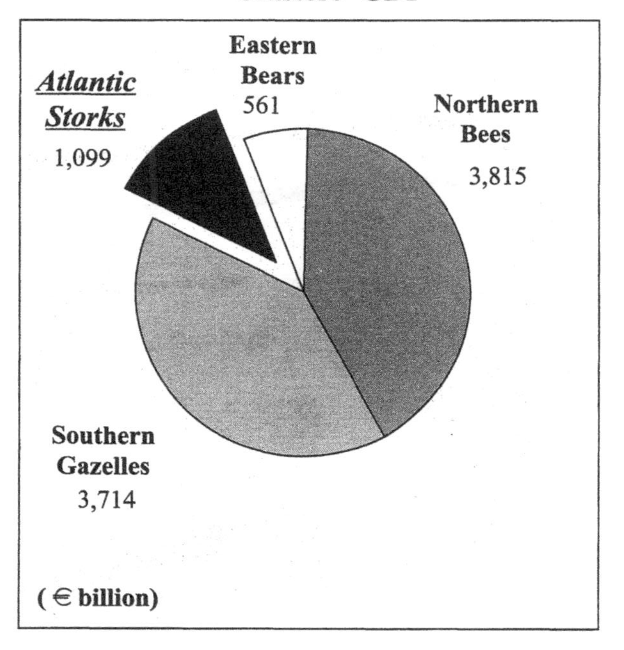

Figure 4.1 Clusters' population and GDP

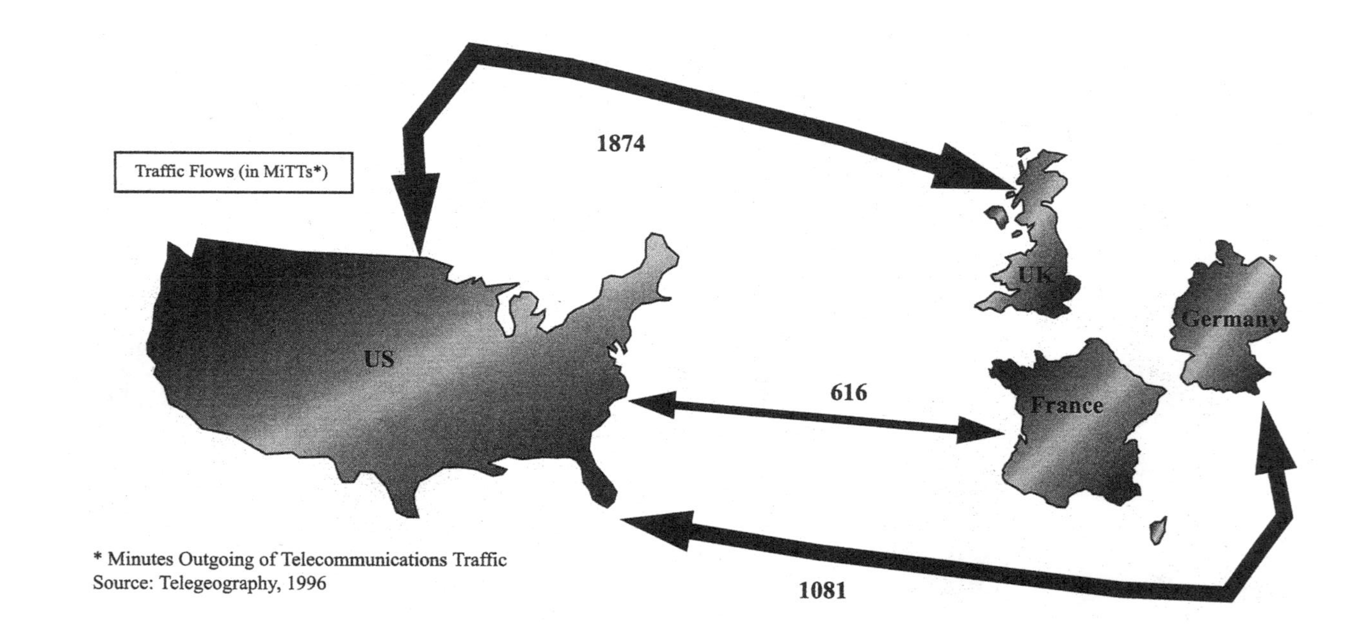

Figure 4.2 The UK is the dominant European telephone link to the USA

Irish governments, which have greatly improved relationships between them. Both governments are united in their desire for a peaceful settlement, and both have given ground to achieve it. As a result, the two countries have become closer and are making a more coherent cluster.

THE ANGLO-AMERICAN CLUSTER

The Storks are blessed and cursed by their language—blessed because English is the language of Europe, and cursed because this has meant they have been under less pressure to adapt to Europe's polyglot culture than other Europeans. As their name implies, the Atlantic Storks have looked to America for international relationships, and Americans have courted them as English-speaking, culturally compatible bridgeheads into a foreign continent. The Storks' international telecommunications are dominated by transatlantic traffic and they are much the largest European destination for incoming calls from North America. Although a third of the size of the Northern Bees cluster, in population terms, the volume of their telecommunication traffic with the USA is 60% higher (Figure 4.2).

INVESTMENT

Investment flows also show the strength of the Atlantic Storks' relationship with the USA. Despite the cluster's small size, it attracts almost three times as much North American investment as Germany, which is the next most favored European country (see Figure 4.3).

The Storks reciprocate—they have invested almost as much in the USA, in recent years as they have in Europe, while Germany and France both invested roughly three times as much in other European countries, as they did in the USA (see Figure 4.4). If anything, these differences in investment flows are widening.

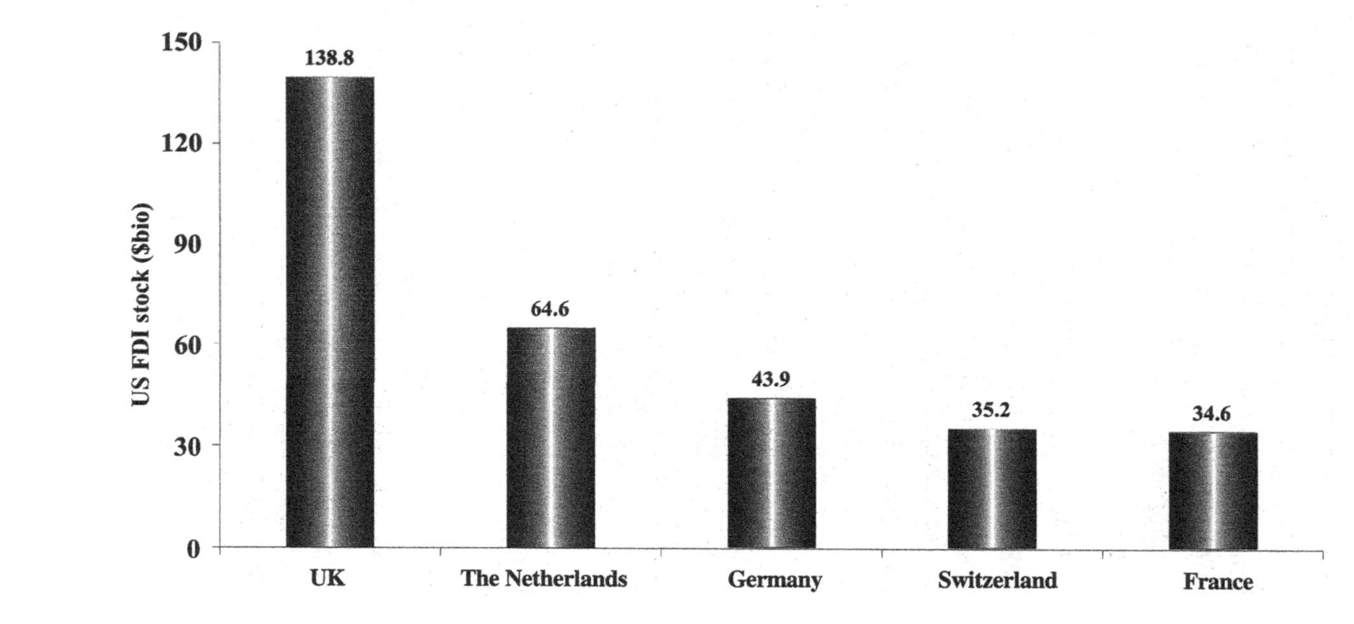

Source: OECD, International Direct Investment Statistics Yearbook 1999

Figure 4.3 The UK is the major destination of US investment in Europe

The UK has invested almost as much in the US as it has in Europe while Germany and France invested much more in Europe than in the US...

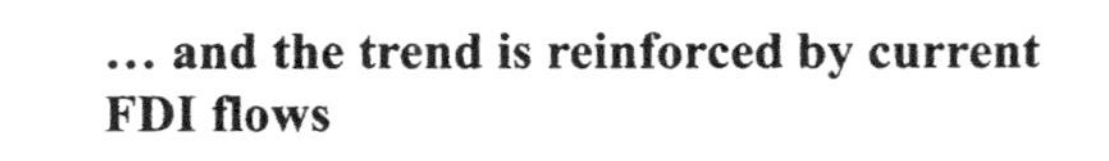

... and the trend is reinforced by current FDI flows

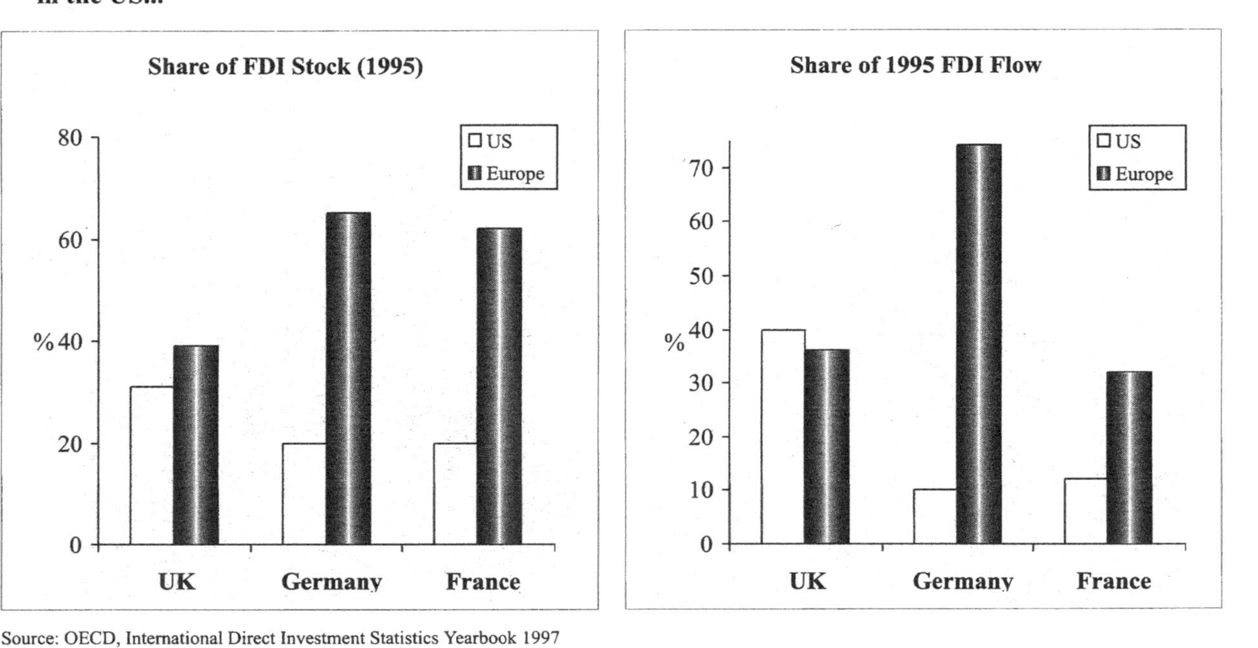

Figure 4.4 Investment in US and Europe by the UK, Germany and France

BRITAIN VS. EUROPE

Such strong investment flows have even prompted some 'Eurosceptics' in the UK to suggest that Britain ought to relinquish its EU membership altogether, and throw in its lot with NAFTA. Such a move would be seen as tantamount to becoming a state of America and be dismissed as absurd and outrageous in every other European country and by the majority of British electors, who have expressed their support for EU membership in a referendum.

Many poke fun at the Anglo-American relationship, and talk of 'two peoples divided by a common language'. However, an apocryphal newspaper headline: 'Fog in the Channel, the continent is isolated' is a more appropriate jest, because the Channel has been a wider cultural barrier than the Atlantic. It may not remain so. The tunnel under the Channel is a cultural, as well as a physical link, because, by removing the possibility that the continent can be 'isolated', it removes a subtle, psychological barrier to the development of closer relationships between the Storks and their continental neighbors. It will be many years, however, before the Storks shift their allegiance, and become whole-hearted members of the European community. History as well as water separates them and although many of the marks of their separate development seem trivial in isolation, their cumulative effect is significant.

It is easy to forget that at the beginning of the 20th century, barely 100 years ago, Britain was the most powerful nation in the world. In 1947, British exports were five times those of France and greater than the combined exports of France, Germany and Italy. The Commonwealth was still an economic power to be reckoned with in those days, and although Churchill foresaw the emergence of the United States of Europe, he felt Britain should position herself at the intersection of three circles: Europe, America and the Commonwealth. This lack of full-hearted commitment to Europe has led the British to miss opportunities to be at the core of the development of major European projects. The other Europeans muse that the British always join five years later, missing the chance to make a major contribution. With the Commonwealth gone as an economic force, they still vacillate between Europe and an America that sees them as just a convenient bridge to Europe.

The risks of this indecision were clearly identified by Sir Nicholas Henderson, when leaving his post as British ambassador in Paris. "Our decline in relation to our European partners," he said "has been so marked that today we are not only no longer a world power, but we are not in the first rank even as a European one." As a former world power, the British find it difficult to accept that 'Brussels' (often seen as a thinly disguised way of saying the Germans or French) should give them direction, and fail to realize that to become European, is not to become German or French. In the words of Lester Thurow: "to be German, one must cease to be English. But no European now exists. It is a beast that has yet to be genetically engineered. When engineered, it will not require an either or choice. One will be able to become an Englishman and a European."

ISOLATED BY ECCENTRICITIES

One of the great strengths of Europe, which is likely to give it a significant economic advantage over other continents, as it becomes integrated, is its cultural pluralism. Each nation and each cluster of nations has qualities the others lack and energy is always released when such differences interact with each other. No one wants or expects Europe to become a monoculture as it integrates, but cultures can be too different, as well as too similar. It is easy to feel the Atlantic Storks as so very different from other European peoples that they are at a disadvantage. In the 1950s, Britain refused at first to join the Common Market, the precursor of the EU. It then joined much later, after it was kept out for many years by General de Gaulle's veto. It then refused to join the Economic and Monetary Union (EMU), and withdrew from the pre-monetary union exchange rate mechanism (ERM) in 1993. It negotiated exemption from the Schengen passport-free travel area. It has only partially adopted the metric system. It clings to its GMT time zone and right-hand drive for cars. Its quarantine laws for pets are unique in Europe. It has very different legal and political systems. These are not mere idiosyncrasies. They have economic consequences.

The 1998 tri-annual survey of international foreign exchange markets by the Bank for International Settlements showed that the London market's daily turnover exceeded the total of the next three largest markets: New York, Tokyo and Singapore. But it is clear that the advent of the euro is undermining this clear supremacy: Frankfurt is growing fast because the British have been reluctant to relinquish sterling in favor of the new common currency. London is and is likely to remain the main market for the US dollar, but the US dollar's status as the main international currency will be challenged by the euro before long. Had Britain been part of European economic and monetary union at the start, London's chances of achieving the same dominant position in the euro market as it enjoys in the dollar market would have been greater. London would also have been a strong candidate for the location of the ECB (European Central Bank) which went to Frankfurt, and Frankfurt traders would probably not have won such a large share of the euro futures market at London's expense.

The Storks' insistence on driving their cars on the left-hand side of the road also has economic consequences. It increases the number of accidents when the Irish and the British drive on the continent, and when continental Europeans visit the UK and Ireland, and it reduces the scale economies for the car industry. Britain's paranoia about rabies, and the draconian quarantine law associated with it, deters pet-loving continental holidaymakers. Its precedent-based system of law adds complexity and cost to European businesses used to codify systems.

And when other Europeans take their computer, portable telephone or hair-dryer from the continent to the UK, they also need to take the massive three pin adapter (now larger than their micro-portable phone) to be able to use the British electric sockets. (Alternatively, they occasionally use the Gazelles adapter: a paper clip or a small key in the top pin isolates the 'foolproof' British safety system ...)

These and many more 'eccentricities' taken together add a certain charm to the Storks, but there is no doubt that they have negative economic consequences. They can be summed up by saying that the British are 'reluctant' Europeans. The Irish are more positive about, and have benefited more financially from EU membership, but the British are tentative and always late. It is not just a British problem, however. It is a problem for the whole of Europe, too. The chances of the euro being introduced smoothly, without too many problems, for instance, would have been greater, had those preparing for the euro's introduction had more access to British input and the formidable financial expertise concentrated in London. It is true that the Storks gain from their close relationship with the USA, and that Europe as a whole derives benefits from their role as mediators between the two continents. However, it is likely that the UK would gain even more from its relationship with America if it were a less reluctant European.

STORKS CULTURE

It is tempting to see the Storks, particularly Britain, as in a similar position, relative to Europe, as Quebec is, relative to the rest of Canada and North America. But the Storks are in no danger of becoming as isolated as Quebec. Their lack of linguistic accomplishments does not isolate them as much as Quebec's Francophone policies, because English is the world's and Europe's second language. The Storks have their own Quebecs, however, in Scotland, Wales and Northern Ireland, which have their own assemblies and reflect a general, pan-European decline in the importance of nation-states. As Europe emerges as a coherent political entity, its members are losing their coherence, and beginning to break up. One of the reasons the IRA and the Basque separatists have declared cease-fires, is that the nation states that were their enemies are becoming absorbed into a super-state, in which traditional regional cultures have more freedom to assert themselves. They can travel freely, without passports, from Spain and France and back. When eventually the only army they could be drafted into is a European army, even the most passionate Basque separatists will begin to wonder whether there is anything left to fight about.

One of the most distinctive cultural features of the Storks is the importance they attach to the freedom of the individual. In this cluster whatever is not prohibited, is permitted. It is the other way round elsewhere in Europe. The emphasis is symbolized by the fact that although Britain is one of the oldest countries in Europe, it doesn't even have a written constitution. This strong, liberal tradition has led to a distaste for laws and regulations, but a general willingness to abide by them, an efficient and honest civil service and bureaucrats who tend to use their common sense, rather than 'go by the book'.

There was a time during the 1960s and 1970s, when the British seemed to be moving closer to the social democratic model of society common in Europe, but, in 1979, the liberal tradition reasserted itself, and the Conservative Party under Margaret Thatcher was decisively returned to power. The subsequent wholesale dismantling of the edifice of social democracy has made the Storks attractive to business. Labor is cheaper and more flexible, social security costs are lower and union power is weaker than in the rest of Europe, making it is easier to fire non-performing or surplus employees. Far from being the problem envisaged in the rest of Europe, where it is seen as endangering social peace, this flexibility means more people are hired—Britain enjoys one of the lowest levels of unemployment in Europe.

The emphasis Thatcherism placed on free and efficient markets has spread to capital markets. Britain was the first European country to embrace the philosophy of shareholder value, and even German investors have looked enviously at the effects on the value creation performance of British companies, compared with their own.

Although Margaret Thatcher lost her job because she was unable to see the importance of Europe to the well-being of Britain, she made a major contribution to the development in Europe of a desire to 'roll back the state', and create more space for individual initiative and risk-taking. In this, at least, the Storks have led the way—all European countries are now privatizing and de-regulating furiously and the election of left-of-center governments in France, Britain and Germany shows no sign of reversing the trend towards free and efficient European markets.

5

The Southern Gazelles—France, Belgium, Italy, Spain, Portugal, Greece, the Balkan countries, Turkey, Bulgaria, Romania

With well over 300 million people, the Southern Gazelles have the largest combined population of Europe's four clusters and cover the second largest land area. Their combined GDP, at 40% of greater Europe's total, is less than that of the Northern Bees, however, which is only two-thirds as populous (see Figure 5.1).

This cluster is not dominated by one country, in the same way the Bees are dominated by Germany or the Storks are dominated by the UK, but France is clearly a 'primus inter pares' among the cluster's 'big four' countries: France, Italy, Spain and Turkey. The primacy of France is evident not only in its GDP which is the largest in the cluster, but also in many other indicators of financial, industrial and technological sophistication. It is home to far more of Europe's top 500 companies than any other cluster member, its stock market capitalization is more than that of Italy's and Spain's combined (see Figure 5.2), and its industries are more efficient. In the 1997 edition of the IMD *World Competitiveness Yearbook*, France ranks 19, ahead of Spain at 25 and Italy at 34. The Yearbook notes that France's strongest assets are science and technology and its degree of internationalization.

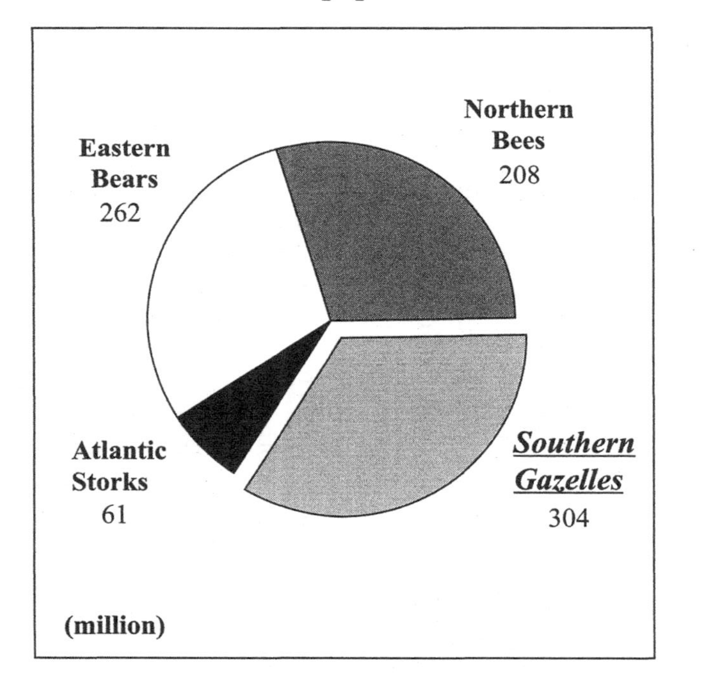

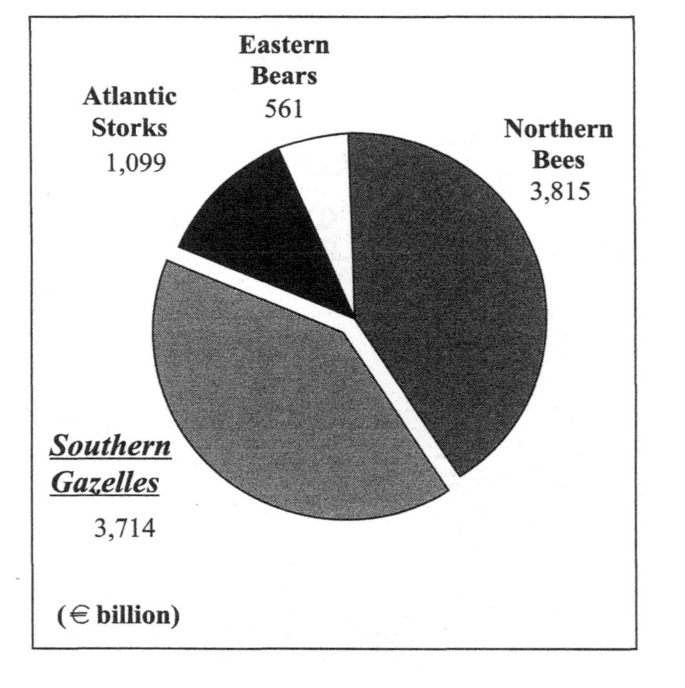

Figure 5.1 Clusters' population and GDP

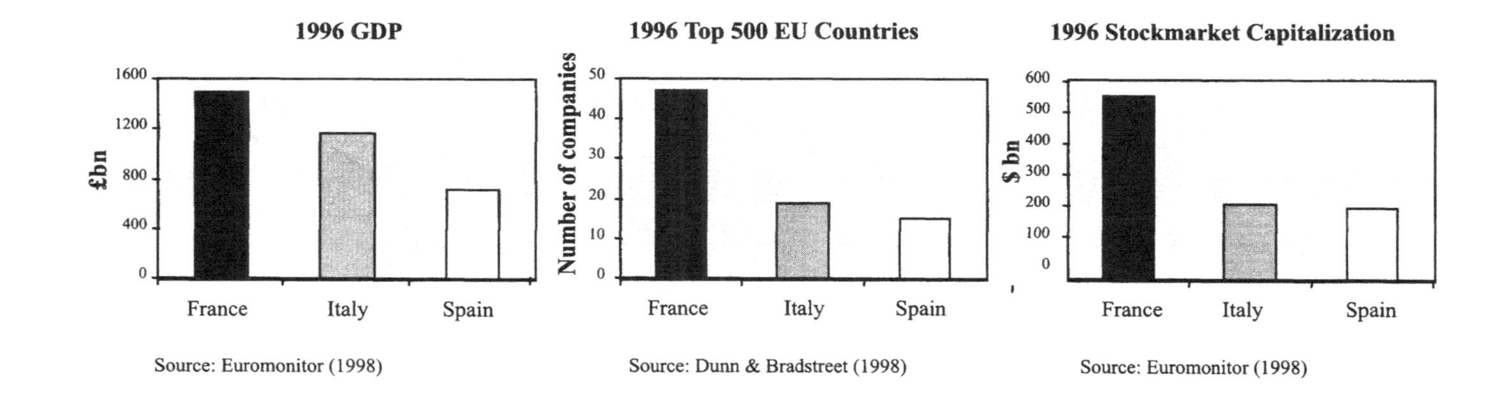

Figure 5.2 Primacy of France among the Gazelles

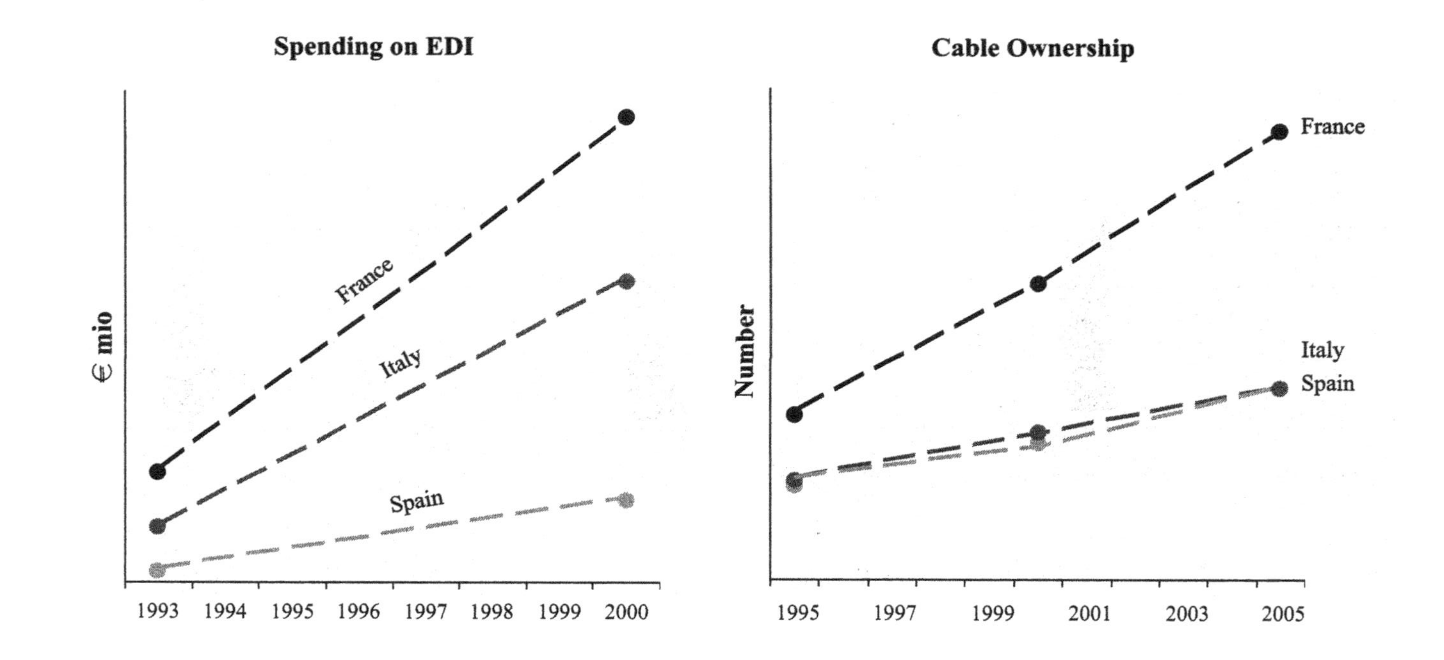

Figure 5.3 Forecasts for EDI and cable ownership

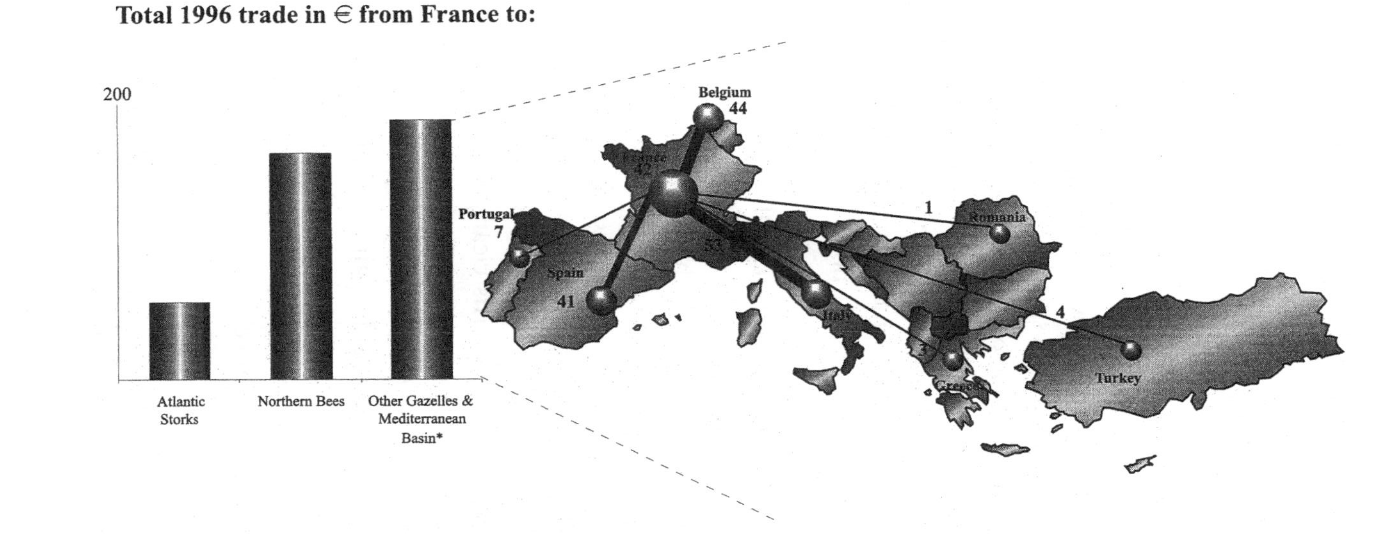

Figure 5.4 France has particularly strong trade links with Belgium, Italy and Spain

Forecasts for electronic data interchange (EDI) spending, and cable ownership (see Figure 5.3), show that France is already and is likely to continue to be much more 'wired', as the modern parlance has it, than its fellow Gazelles.

TRADE AND INVESTMENT

France has particularly strong trade links with Italy, Spain, and Belgium, but, as Figure 5.4 shows, it also trades actively with the Northern Bees, and the Atlantic Storks. One of the most significant developments in the Gazelles cluster, in recent years, has been a rapid strengthening of economic ties between France and Spain. Trade between the two countries has grown at almost 10% a year throughout the 1990s and France is now Spain's most important trading partner.

Patterns of foreign direct investment also show a far greater strengthening of links between France and Spain, than between France and Italy. The reason why the French retail industry's invasion of the Spanish retail industry has succeeded so well (see below) is that consumer preferences in the two countries are very similar. The Alps, it seems, have been significantly less permeable economically and culturally, than the Pyrenees (see Figure 5.5). But overall trade and investment patterns clearly indicate an emergent cluster, that is beginning to embrace, although with considerably less enthusiasm than the Northern Bees, its main eastern neighbors. Trade between France, Italy and Spain, on the one hand, and Romania, Bulgaria and Turkey, on the other, has grown faster than the trade of those three eastern European countries with Germany, Russia and the UK (see Figure 5.6).

INVESTMENT

The same trends are evident in investment. In 1995, five of the eight favorite countries for French foreign investment were Gazelles, and as Figure 5.7 shows, the big three—France, Italy and Spain—

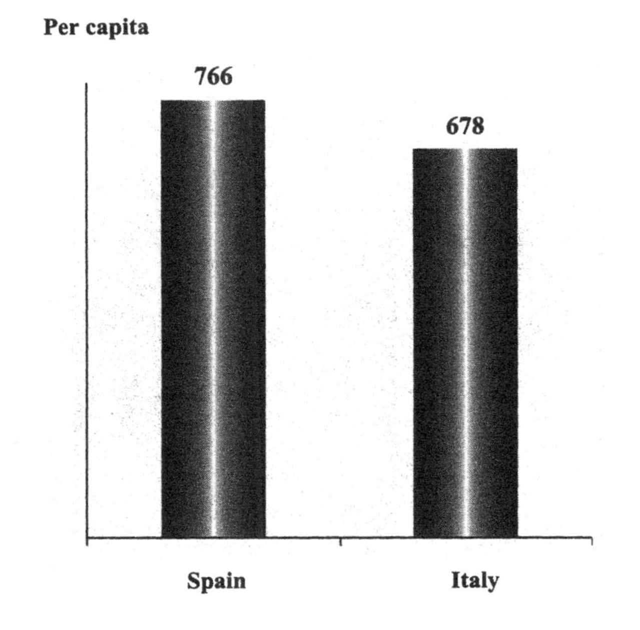

Source: Monthly Statistics of Foreign Trade 1999, OECD
International Direct Investment Statistics year 1998, OECD

Figure 5.5 Links between France and Spain are greater than between France and Italy

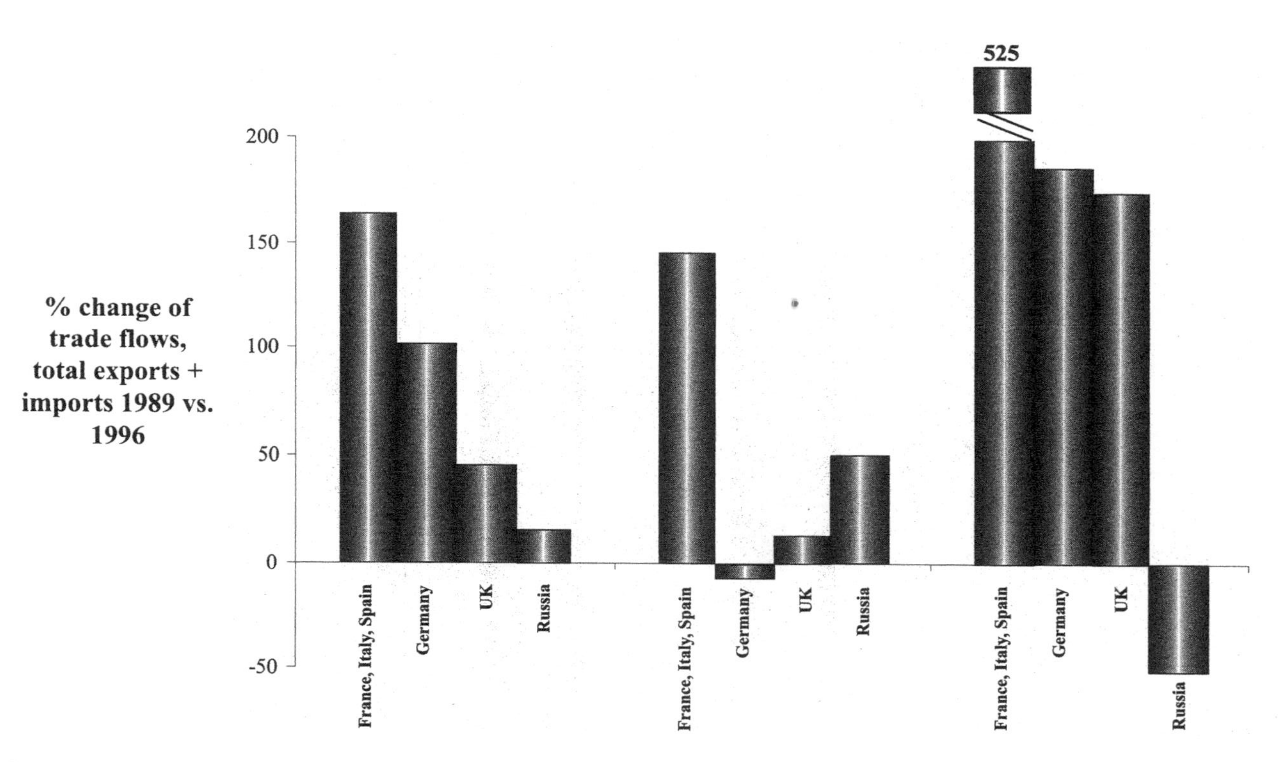

Source: Direction of trade statistics yearbook 1996, IMF

Figure 5.6 Southern Gazelles' top trade countries: growth of trade 1989–1996

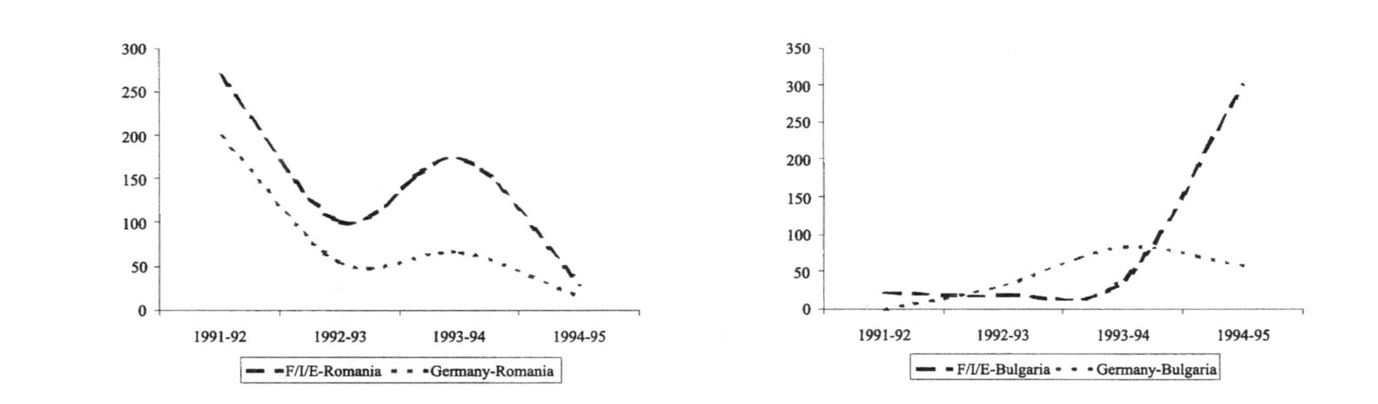

Source: OECD, International Direct Investment Statistics yearbook, 1997

Figure 5.7 1991–95 FDI flow trends into Romania and Bulgaria (France, Italy, Spain, Germany)

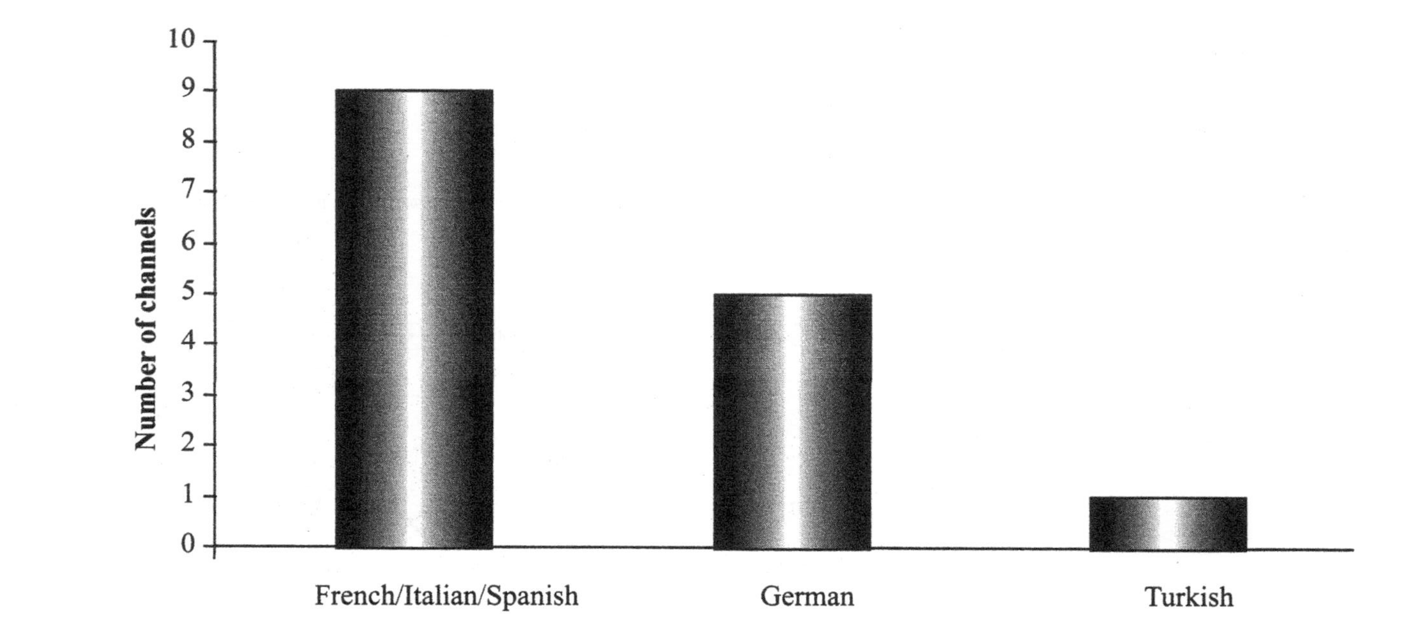

Source: Television 97.

Figure 5.8 Foreign channel penetration – Romania

have been consistently investing more in Romania than has Germany, and have recently shown a particularly strong appetite for Bulgarian assets.

CULTURE AND INDUSTRY

French is the predominant third language within the cluster. However, because the Germans like to vacation on sunny beaches, German remains popular in Spain, Portugal, Slovenia and Croatia. Russian is still dominant in Bulgaria. Almost all of the languages spoken in the cluster have Latin roots. Latin is the basis of Romania's language, so it is no surprise that Romanians have become avid watchers of French, Italian and Spanish television channels (see Figure 5.8). It is the similarity of language, as much as proximity, that has made Romania so attractive to literally thousands of Italian entrepreneurs as a place to establish very small joint ventures.

The importance of tourism for this climate-blessed cluster is another of its distinctive features. France, Spain and Italy have Europe's largest national tourist industries in terms of numbers of visitors. Indeed if industry is the characteristic economic activity of the Bees, and services (and particularly financial services) are the strong suit of Storks, tourism is where the Gazelles excel. The strength of France's retail industry is also distinctive. All but 3% of the French food retailing industry is in French hands, over half of the supermarkets in Spain and Portugal are owned by French chains, and French retailers are busy buying into supermarket chains in Italy, through joint ventures. The Gazelles also differ sharply from other clusters in their high incidence of labor disputes. Greece and Spain, with 87, and 84 days a year lost per thousand population respectively, during 1993–95, were the worst afflicted, but Italy lost 45 days, Portugal lost 13 and France lost 10 (see Figure 5.9).

Perhaps it's the wine. Of Europe's top six countries in terms of wine consumption per head, five are Gazelles (see Figure 5.10). Could there be something significant in the correlation between

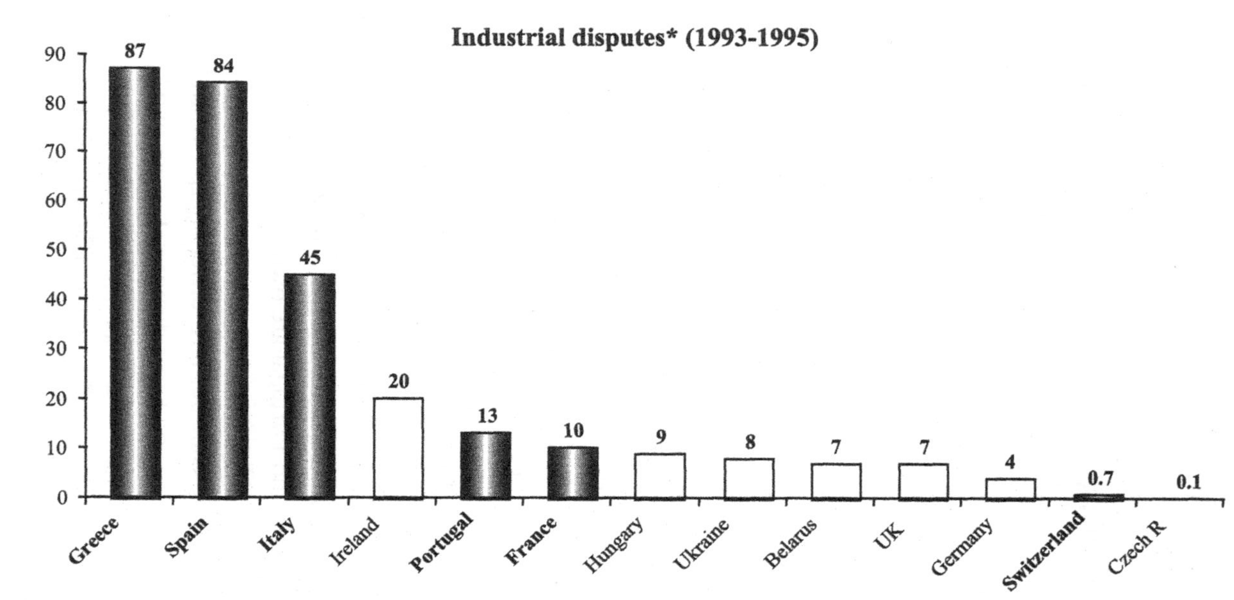

Figure 5.9 Strikes and lockouts are strongly influenced by the Latin culture leading to a very high number of days not worked in contrast to the Northern countries

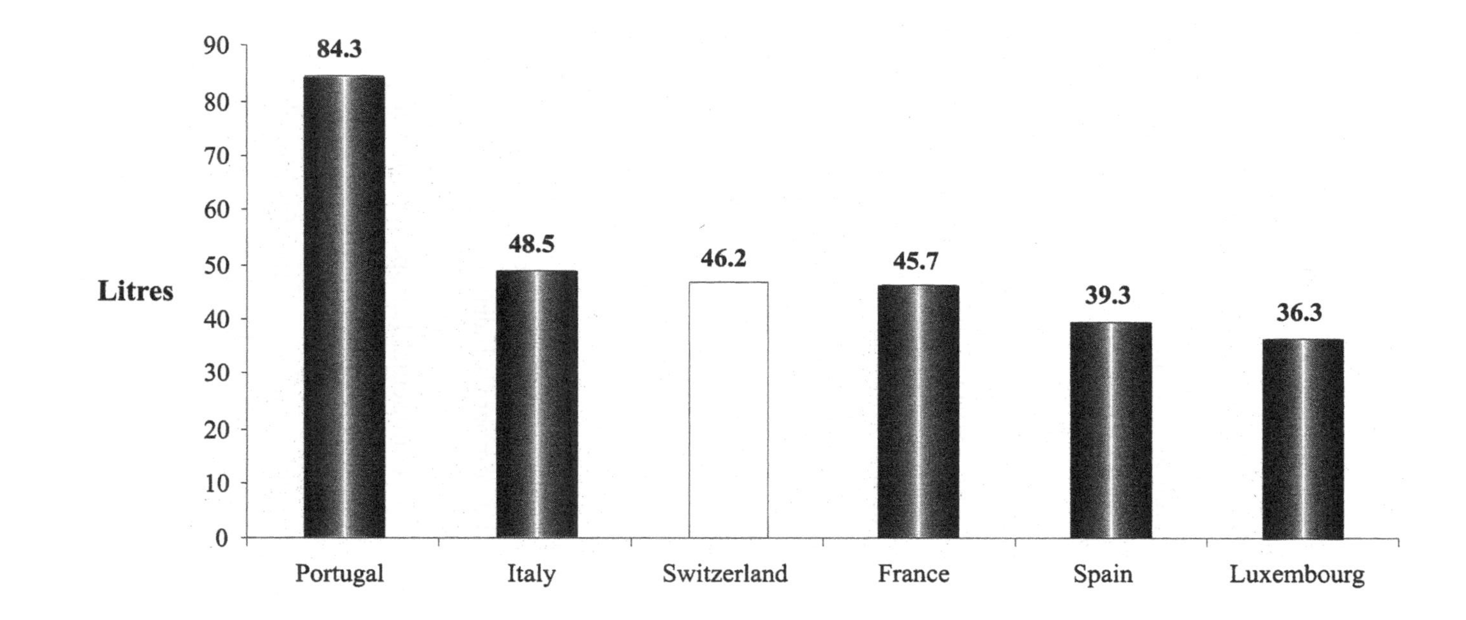

Source: Eurocentre

Figure 5.10 Per capita consumption of wine — Europe's top six (1997)

beer-drinking and low incidence of industrial disputes, and wine-drinking and high incidence? Will Bees and Storks employees become increasingly belligerent as they drink more wine, and Gazelles become more compliant as they drink more beer? Or is there something more deeply-rooted in the psyche of Gazelles, that makes them such troublesome employees?

THE GAZELLES' WAY OF LIFE

A glance at the list of laws, regulations and rules that most Gazelles societies live under, might give the impression these are very regimented societies, with a strong sense of social duty. But despite all the rules, or perhaps, in a subtle way, because of them, the opposite is the case, as it is in Eastern Bears societies. Everything that is not permitted, is in theory prohibited in Gazelles societies. Its citizens are supposed to follow the rules, but half the time they do not know them, the rules often contradict each other, and people spend a lot of time seeking 'off the record' advice from officials on how to get round them. It is a very individualistic cluster. Everyone is an exception in most Gazelles societies, and there is very little sense of community. In the USA, most people give their time and money generously to good causes, and in the UK, some 80% of SC Johnson Wax employees are involved in community work in one way or another. At the company's Italian operations, however, the figure is only 10%. One reason for these contrasts is that the social democratic countries of continental Europe have developed more elaborate welfare states than the USA or the UK, but there is more to it than that in the Gazelles cluster.

The prevailing philosophies are 'every man for himself', and 'get away with as much as you can'. It is always open season on bureaucrats, and particularly tax officials. The idea that evading tax is immoral, because it imposes additional burdens on others, is quite alien to Gazelles societies where tax evasion is a symbol of virility. Tax rates are significantly higher in Gazelles countries, but the proportions of GDP accounted for by tax revenues are not that much higher than in the nominally much less heavily taxed UK. No stigma is attached to evading taxes or being active in the 'black economy', just as no stigma is attached to other forms of what Anglo-Saxons would deem immorality. President Clinton risked impeachment for lying about his sexual peccadilloes. Former French President, the late Francois Mitterand, made no secret of his illegitimate child, and French newspapers saw no story in the fact.

France is unusual within the cluster in having a long tradition of public service, and good administration by an elite corps of officials, trained at its 'Grandes Ecoles'. Spain and Italy, are less capable in this area, and public institutions are less respected, and generally more corrupt. Strenuous efforts are now being made in all Gazelles countries (particularly those that are already in, or wish to join the EU) to improve the quality and status of their administrative institutions. It is now widely recognized within Gazelles countries that extensive public ownership and excessive rules and regulations, inhibit the entrepreneurial activity that is so vital to an adaptable modern economy. Spain, Italy and even France have started with gusto to privatize former 'public' services such as telecoms, airlines, energy, banking and insurance companies.

The Mediterranean, the cradle of western civilization and the artery of early commerce, is an important unifying feature of the Gazelles cluster. Mussolini regarded Italy as the aircraft carrier of the Mediterranean, because of its central position and its proximity to northern Africa. Just as the Storks link Europe with America, so the Gazelles link Europe with Africa and the Middle East and straddle the border between Christendom and Islam. The proximity of the southern Gazelles to the Middle East and the Maghreb, and the sea-borne commerce that has linked all of the countries on the Mediterranean rim together for literally thousands of years, makes the Gazelles more 'exposed' to non-European cultures than the other three clusters. To the poor, hungry masses in the Maghreb, Europe is Italy, Spain and France and holds a deep fascination. It is the equivalent of the USA for the Mexicans. The steady stream of immigrants from the south has been joined, in recent years, by an influx from the east. Thousands of Albanians have been flooding into Italy, from across the Adriatic.

THE EASTERN GAZELLES

Of the former Soviet bloc countries only Bulgaria and Romania are of much interest from a business point of view, and as we have seen above, their integration with Europe, through trade and direct foreign investment, is already under way. The Balkan countries are too small, too poor, and too ravaged by ethnic conflicts to be significant factors in deciding how companies should organize themselves. All the indications are that they will be linked more closely with the Gazelles, than the Northern Bees, but if it turns out otherwise, it will not matter much.

Turkey is much more significant, however. With its high inflation, corrupt officials, and often violent problems with its Kurdish minority, Turkey seems remote from the European mainstream. Its strategic importance, as the southern flank of NATO, has declined sharply since the break-up of the Soviet Union. Moreover, Greece, at present the eastern-most member of the EU, has been at daggers drawn with the Turks for most of this century, partly because of their long-running dispute over Cyprus, but largely because Greece used to be part of the Ottoman Empire, governed from Istanbul. Greek memories of the much-resented Ottoman dominance, remain fresh and sour its relationship with its much larger neighbor. Following the dismemberment of the Ottoman Empire in 1923 at the Treaty of Lausanne, and the subsequent emergence of a Turkish republic under Kemal Ataturk, however, Turkey has become more westernized. Ataturk adopted the Roman alphabet, and demanded that Turkish men and women put away the fez and the veil. The eagerness with which Turkey has sought membership of the EU is a legacy of the Ataturk reforms and reflects the desire of the Turks to align themselves with their western neighbors. The process of integration will take many years, but with 60 million people, Turkey has the largest population of all the Gazelles and its economy is growing fast. It cannot be ignored—it is eastern Europe's sleeping giant, and a rapidly growing market for the western goods that already fill the shops of Istanbul and Ankara. Turkey is also Europe's gateway to Asia, through the remnants of the Ottoman Empire. Beyond it to the north and east of the Caspian Sea, lie the " 'Stans" (the former Soviet Islamic republics of Kazakhistan, Uzbekistan, Turkmenistan, etc.) which, though sparsely populated are rich in oil and gas and are likely, in time, to become an important source of energy for Europe.

The Southern Gazelles are a less homogeneous cluster than the other three, but they are more integrated economically and emotionally with the rest of Europe than the Atlantic Storks, and pose a less formidable management challenge than those alarmingly disorganized and crisis-prone economies that comprise the Eastern Bears.

6

The Eastern Bears—Russia, Ukraine, Belarus

"I cannot forecast to you the actions of Russia," British Prime Minister, Winston Churchill, famously acknowledged, during a radio broadcast in 1939. "It is a riddle wrapped in a mystery inside an enigma." Six decades later, Russia is less of a riddle and its mystery is fading, but its future in the short and medium term remains an enigma. Given that the Eastern Bears produce today barely half the output of the Atlantic Storks, it may be hard to believe that in the long term they will become a very important and powerful part of the European economy (see Figure 6.1). Yet there is no doubt that this will happen.

The three Bears are a very coherent cluster, not just because local languages were outlawed during the Soviet hegemony when Russian was enforced as the first language in all three countries, but also because their people still share a sense of destiny. All suffered together under the inefficient Soviet system and all are equally poor. Moreover, they are not as attracted by the culture and life style of western Europe as the Poles, Czechs or Hungarians. Even during the worse recent economic crisis less than one in five Russians was thinking of emigrating if the situation deteriorated any further. And as a recent survey of Ukrainian adults showed, political independence has done little to weaken their belief that their future lies in closer links with Russia, and other former Soviet Union (CIS—Confederation of Independent States) countries (see Figure 6.2).

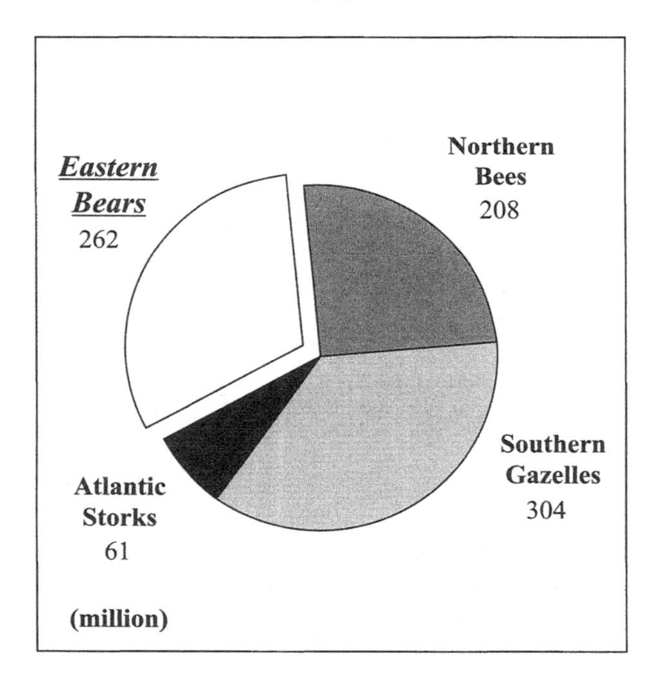

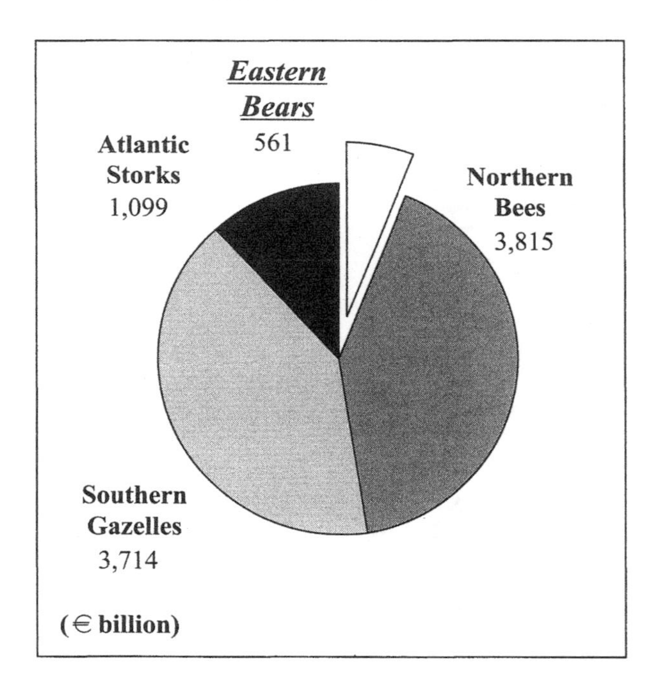

Figure 6.1 Clusters' population and GDP

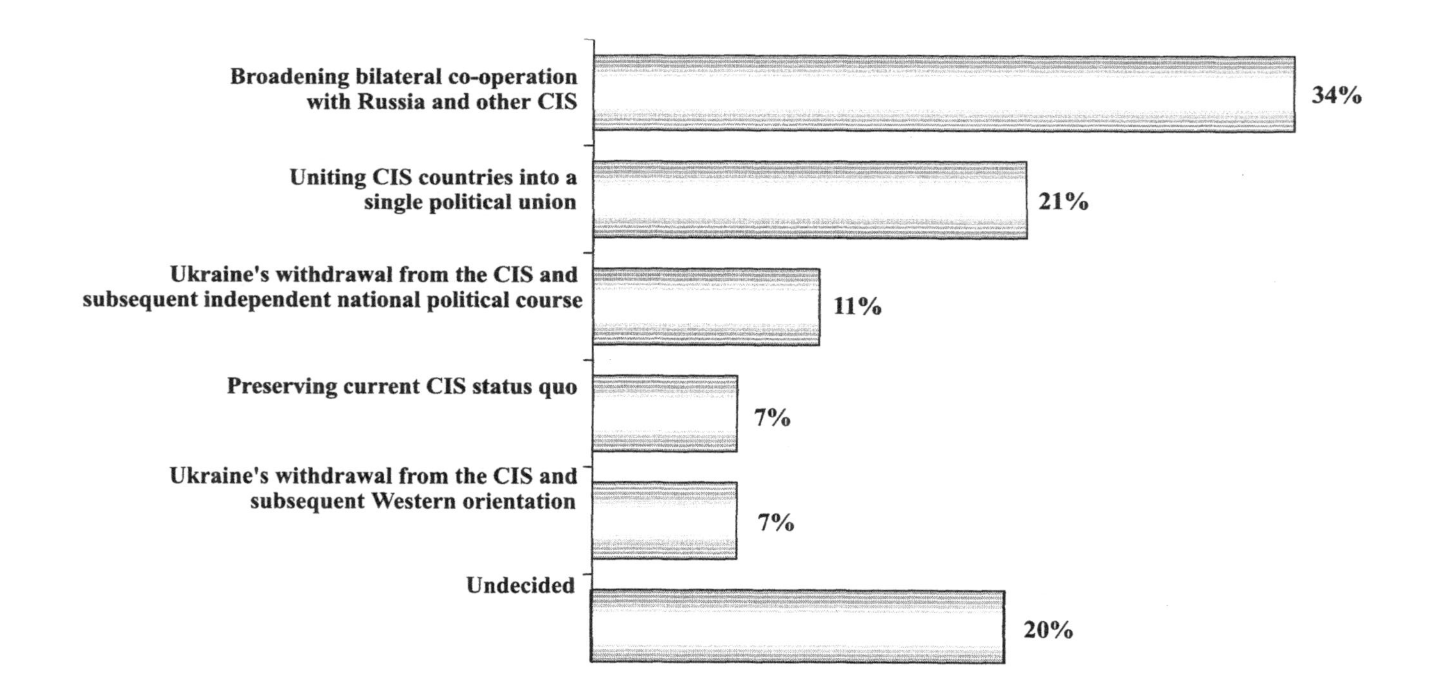

Figure 6.2 In 1998, 2015 Ukrainian adults were asked: "Which of the following political positions would you describe as best for the Ukraine?"

In view of these feelings of solidarity with the old imperial power, many people were surprised when a tide of nationalism, beginning in central Europe, and then spreading to the Baltic states, the Caucasus, Ukraine and Belarus, dismembered the Soviet Union in just a few years. It became apparent that these countries had never been willingly parts of the Russian Empire, and had always harbored a yearning for independence. Ukraine initially became united with Russia at about the same time that Scotland joined England, 300 years ago. But, like the Scots, Ukrainians hankered for their lost independence and reclaimed it as soon as the opportunity presented itself. The separation of Ukraine from Russia was of considerable interest to the West, because of the Soviet missile bases on Ukrainian territory. Anxious to accelerate the process of demilitarization, the West courted Ukraine assiduously, and invited it to participate in NATO's military exercises, under the Partnership for Peace program. Despite such attempts to re-align it with the West, however, Ukraine, particularly its eastern flank, remains much closer, culturally, to Russia than to western Europe. For its part, the Belarus government is still so devoted to its former political masters, it wants to use the sickly Russian ruble as its official currency.

The cultural affinity, binding the Eastern Bears together, is being cemented by increasingly close economic bonds. Under the eastern common market system (CMEA or Comecon) of Soviet days, each country produced the goods assigned to it. Plants would receive raw materials from other Comecon plants, and export their output throughout the Comecon. In this way, strong trade links were established among factories that have survived the collapse of the USSR. During 1988–95, Russia's trade with Belarus and Ukraine (the value of imports, plus exports) increased by 75%, compared to the increase of less than 15% in its trade with the other three European clusters.

A SENSE OF INSECURITY

For a marketer, much the most obvious geographical feature of the Eastern Bears cluster is its enormous size, stretching all the way from the Baltic to Vladivostok in the Far East, just a short sea journey from Japan. However, it is not a feature of much commercial significance. During the Second World War Russia developed cities such as Novosibirsk and Krasnoyarsk, as centers for scientific research and heavy industry and armaments production in the more easily defensible territory east of the Urals. However, some 80% of Russians live west (or within a few hundred kilometers east) of the Urals, and always have done. Russia extends to Japan territorially, but culturally, the countries are poles apart. Russians also feel ill at ease in the Caucasus region between the Black and Caspian seas. It is an important area, because it includes the large oil province around Baku on the Caspian coast, but the minarets and oriental traditions of Azerbaijan, Georgia and Armenia, proclaim their membership of a culture that most Russians understand no better than the Italians and Greeks understand the Turks.

With a population and a territory both comparable to those of the USA, the Bears are certainly large enough to go their own way, as they have for most of the 20th century. However, should they choose, as they now show the intention of doing, to relinquish their insularity, there is no doubt about the direction in which they will lean. Their culture and thus their future are linked inextricably to Europe, and have always been. Historically it has not always been a comfortable association, however, because, until the age of intercontinental ballistic missiles, the lack of any significant mountain ranges between the main centers of population and western Europe made Russia very vulnerable to western European invaders, such as France and Germany. Russians developed a very successful defensive strategy—they let invaders approach Moscow in the summer across hundreds of miles of flat country until their supply lines became over-stretched, held them there until the snow started falling and then waited for 'General Winter' to finish them off. However, their vulnerability made the Russians feel insecure, and led them to impoverish themselves by spending up to 25% of their GNP on defense.

ECONOMIC PROSPECTS

A distinctive feature of this cluster is its huge reserves of hydrocarbons. The former Soviet Union has the world's largest reserves of natural gas—40 trillion cubic meters, compared to the Middle East's 33 trillion—and a significant share of the world's proven oil reserves (see Figure 6.3).

The economic importance of the cluster is further enhanced by its close historical links to the Islamic republics round the Caspian sea, the oil reserves of which are estimated at 15–30 billion barrels (compared to 22 billion barrels in the USA and 17 billion barrels in the North Sea). Kazakhstan accounts for roughly half of the region's total reserves and western oil companies have been buzzing around it, like bees around honey. In 1993, Chevron signed a $20 billion joint venture deal with the Kazakh government, to develop the large Tengiz field, and from 1999, oil has been exported through the Tengiz-Novorossirsk pipeline, owned by the Caspian Pipeline Consortium (CPC). Though no longer part of the Soviet Union, Kazakhstan remains firmly within the Russian sphere of influence. A third of its population is ethnic Russian and Russian remains the official language, spoken by two-thirds of the population. Lest anyone suppose Russia is willing to surrender its position in this oil-rich country, it should be noted that it controls a third of the CPC, both directly and indirectly, through joint ventures with other members, such as LukArco (Russia/UK) and Rosneft-Shell (Russia/UK-Netherlands).

Soaring Russian inflation in the early 1990s moderated and was expected to remain subdued (see Figure 6.4 for a forecast made in 1996) until the 'Asian flu' caused havoc in the weak Russian financial markets in 1998 and forced a major, inflation-fueling devaluation. Such crises will recur periodically in Brazil-style fashion until the Russian government establishes a realistic tax code, and collects enough revenue to cover its budget. In the old days, when everything was state-owned, tax was not an issue. The banks recycled some of the money collected from a company's client back

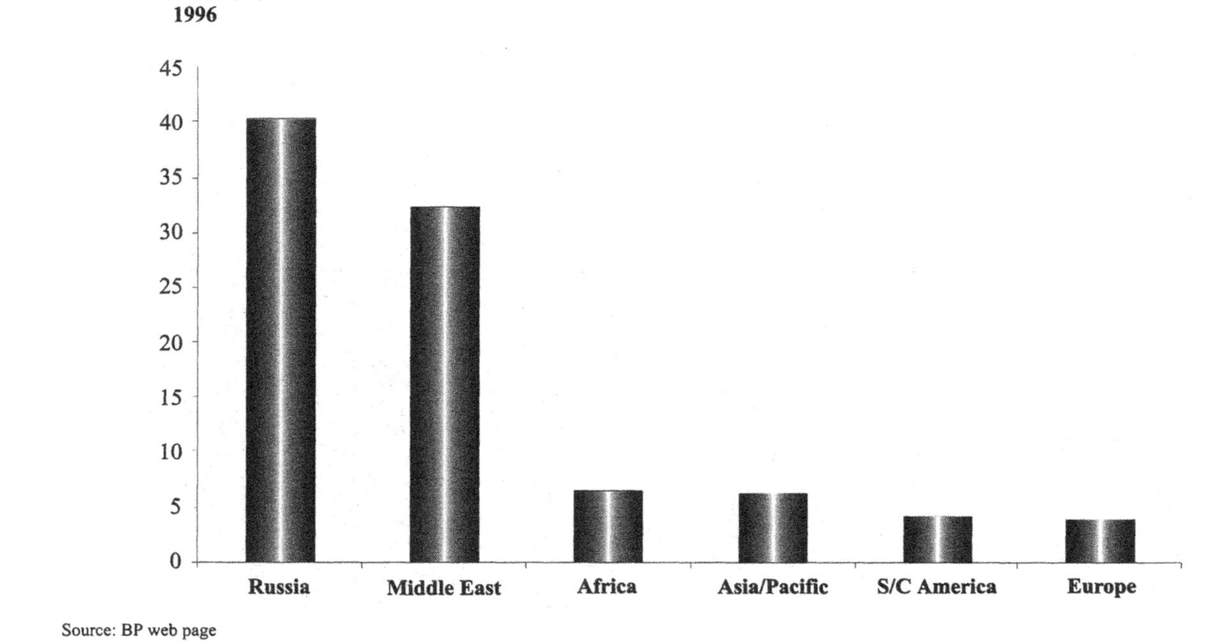

Source: BP web page

Figure 6.3 Russia has the world's largest gas reserves

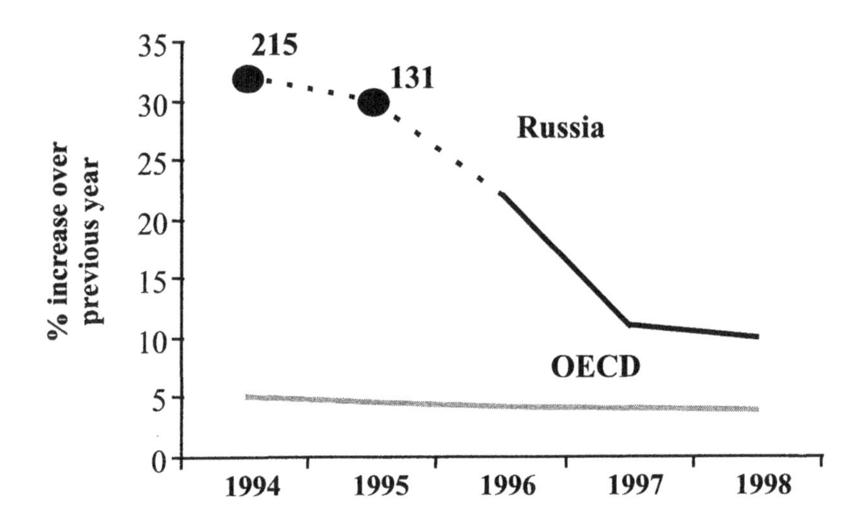

Figure 6.4 Official Russian consumer prices

to the company, and gave the rest to the government. Now that even inefficient state-owned organizations are legal entities responsible for their own profit and loss accounts and balance sheets, taxes need to be assessed and collected. Economic growth was negative until 1997, but has become positive since and is expected to accelerate, despite the fact that, officially, at any rate, cluster unemployment remains very high, relative to the OECD average and is expected to rise (Figure 6.5).

The official unemployment rate should not be a reason for great concern, however, because it only describes the situation in the government-run sector. In Soviet days that was 100% of the economy, but nowadays at least 50% of production goes unreported. Three out of four people working for a major firm say they haven't been paid for weeks or months, yet they do not starve. Figure 6.6 shows how a large subsistence economy keeps the wolf from the Bears' door.

In Soviet times, 80% of the Bears' potato crop and an even larger proportion of the fruit and vegetable crops came from small

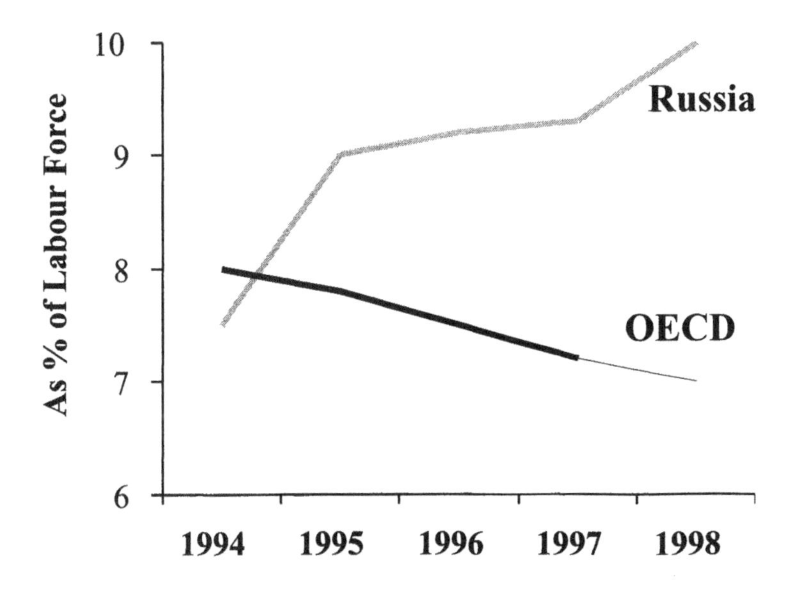

Figure 6.5 Official Russian unemployment

'victory gardens' at 'dachas' (summer houses) to which just 3% of cultivated land was devoted. They are still tended during the summer to supplement expensive foodstuff and to ensure family survival during the harsh winters.

The scale and vitality of the unofficial 'black' economy in this cluster are hopeful signs, because they show that people realize they can no longer rely on politicians, and must fend for themselves (see Figure 6.7). Many of them need two unofficial jobs to supplement their income from their official job to keep themselves alive. Naturally these go unreported (otherwise you will be laid off and lose your place in line, should something good magically happen), and do not appear in any official statistic. This subsistence farming, and the wheeling and dealing required to offset the distortions of hopelessly inefficient labor markets, are creating a habit of self-sufficiency from which entrepreneurial sub-economies are emerging. In the west, most people are self-employed or employed by small firms: in the UK, for instance, firms employing fewer than 20

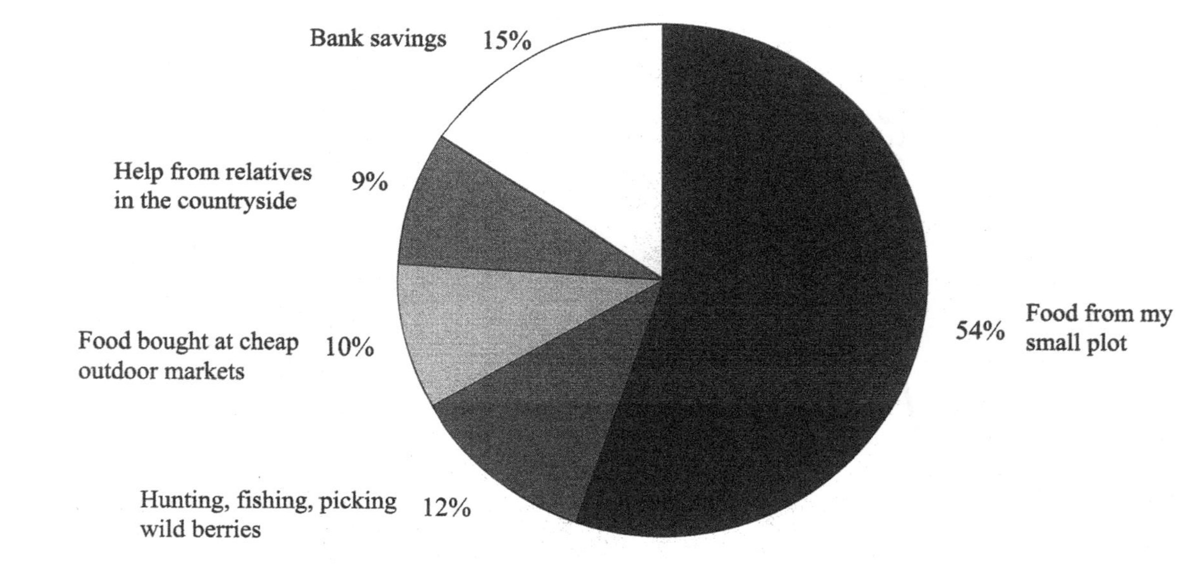

Source: ISM Research Center - 3,340 respondents across Russia, Sept 1998

Figure 6.6 What will enable you to live through the economic crisis?

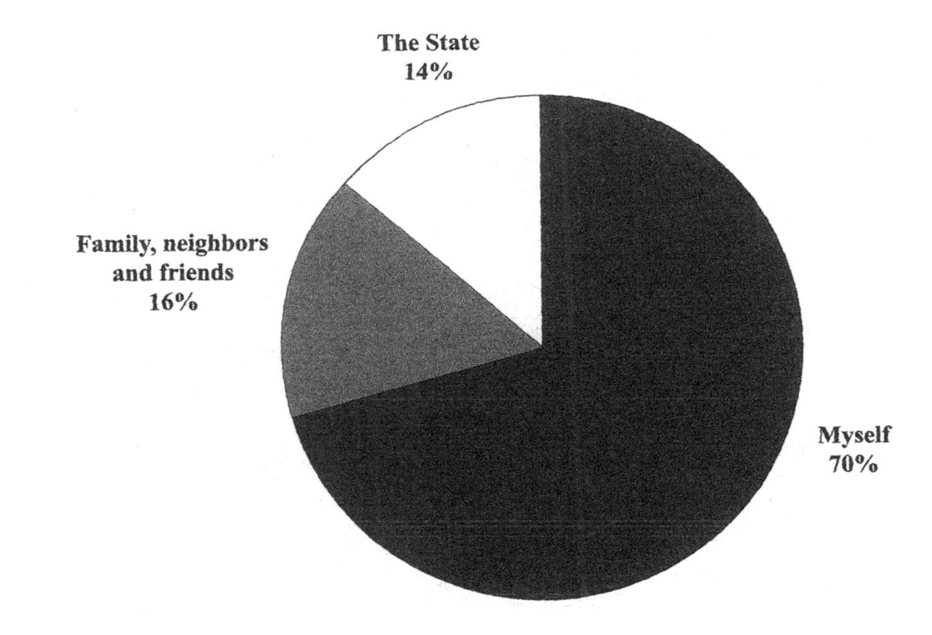

Figure 6.7 On whom are you relying to get through the crisis?

people account for 82% of manufacturing employment. Although not tracked by official figures, similar networks of small firms are emerging within the Eastern Bears, creating unofficial employment for many, and considerable wealth for a few.

The enormous size of the cluster means that the proportion of people involved in this vigorous and increasingly prosperous unofficial segment of the economy need not be high to create a viable market. Just a tenth of the cluster population is equivalent to almost half the size of the UK or France. Signs of this prosperous, westernized minority are increasingly evident in the Russian translations in menus in the luxury resorts of Marbella in Spain and Antibes in France. And the €300 a night Negresco Hotel in Nice reports that Russians normally occupy 8% of its rooms. Its size, its prodigious reserves of oil and gas and its very well educated, though seriously underemployed population (see below), make this a cluster of enormous strategic importance for western firms. It is in a terrible mess in many ways, and its economies have been badly mishandled, but it's in no more of a mess than China was 20 years ago. If western companies had realized then what China would be like today, they would have tried harder to cultivate the managerial ability to deal with her, and thus be in a much stronger position now. They must not make the same mistake with the Eastern Bears.

It's impossible to predict how the Eastern Bears will perform in the future, but it is most likely that their combined GDP will more than double over the next 15 years, increasing sharply their share of total European GDP. Whatever happens—however protracted and painful the transition from communism to capitalism turns out to be—it is hard to see how the combined economies of the Bears could fail to grow by more than 50% during the next 15 years. Consumer spending should grow rapidly up to 2010, and is very likely to have overtaken that of the Atlantic Storks by then, and to be growing at a far faster rate than spending in the rest of greater Europe. The Bears are going to be an important locomotive for the European economy over the next two decades because, despite all the crippling inefficiencies and misallocation of resources inflicted on the people by central planning, communism can lay claim to one shining achievement of enormous economic significance. Before the revolution in 1917, illiteracy rates in the cluster were among the highest in Europe. They are now among the lowest, and the standards of education in math and science are among the best in the world. In the long run, the level of education is the most important determinant of economic potential, but it will probably take decades for the Bears to exploit fully the opportunities with which communism's greatest legacy has endowed them. For there are many much less welcome legacies of the Soviet system that inhibit the realization of the cluster's potential, and cause the priceless asset of very high standards of education to be largely wasted.

THE LEGACY OF ABSURDITIES

Western visitors to Kiev one day in the early 1990s were very alarmed to discover, on their arrival, that the following day the price of bread would be increased by 500% and that, at the same time, bread production would be halved. They assumed the two developments would precipitate a major famine, and lead to serious civil disorder. As they cautiously emerged from their hotels, expecting to be attacked by mobs of angry food rioters, they were pleasantly surprised to find the city quiet, and much as it had been the day before. There were grumbles about the price increase, but the queues outside bakeries were shorter, and people were going about their business calmly and with no apparent concerns about an impending bread shortage. A few inquiries soon established the reason for the strangely cool reaction to the announcements. It lay in the absurdly distorted bread market in Ukraine.

The value chain was conventional enough: farmers harvested their wheat and sold it to the state buying organization. The grain was shipped to the mills, and the flour was then shipped to the bakeries. The absurdity lay in the prices fixed by the state. Before the price rise, bread was so cheap that farmers bought half the output of the bakeries, and fed it to their cattle. The price rise closed this bizarre arbitrage window and wheat became cheaper than bread, so the wise farmers fed wheat and not bread to their cows. Bakeries ceased to be cattle feed producers and their halved output remained adequate for human consumption. Hence the absence of food riots.

Equally absurd was the predicament of a Russian in the old Soviet system of centralized planning who waited in line for half an hour at a store, to buy a pen. When she finally got to the front of the line, she found the shop had run out of pens. However, because she was reluctant to waste her investment in waiting in line, she bought a pencil instead. It was so cheap, anyway. The man behind her had wanted to buy a pencil, but the shop had just sold the last pencil to the woman in front of him, so he had to settle for a cheap pot of glue. The person next in line wanted a pot of glue … and so on.

It was a wonderful market for western companies. All they had to do was to persuade one official, at the relevant ministry, to allow them to distribute their goods to the shops, and the whole shipment would be sold in a few days. The result of the system, however, was that people emerged from the shops with pens, pencils and pots of glue they didn't really want, and started looking for people who did want them. Illegal barter flourished, because it was the only logical way to correct the distortions created by central planning. When money could only buy you things you did not really want, goods themselves became the most important currency. But as everyone knows, money transactions replaced the barter system, because barter was a very inefficient way of matching willing buyers and willing sellers, and frequent shortages of goods were the inevitable consequences of this inefficiency.

In the early days, following the opening up of the previously protected Eastern Bears markets, western consumer goods firms which felt a need for a little market research, would conduct what they called 'pantry checks'. For a small fee, the market researchers could visit a home, open cupboards, and note down their contents. When they found a cupboard full of dozens of bars of soap, and asked the householder why she had so much, she would explain that there was currently a shortage of soap and she could thus barter it for milk at a favorable rate. The flourishing black markets found everywhere in the Eastern Bear economies, were illegal, but were playing a vital role in facilitating the transition from central planning to liberal capitalism. They showed that 'the general disposition to truck, barter, and exchange' that Adam Smith noted in *The Wealth of Nations*, was alive and well in the Eastern Bears economies and struggling vigorously to establish the free market conditions in which it can thrive. Similar, wealth-destroying absurdities survive throughout the Eastern Bears economies. Official figures overstate the levels of unemployment, because the 'black economy' is so large. The real problem, in the cluster's labor markets, is not so much unemployment, as the persistence of an absurd level of underemployment. People who speak three languages make more money driving trucks than teaching. University professors earn more than their monthly salaries teaching foreigners to speak Russian for three of four hours a week, because they're paid for that in dollars or other western currencies.

Like many other Soviet markets, the labor market was, and to a large extent remains, a parody of its western counterparts. In the old days, the common joke was 'they pretend to pay us, and we pretend to work', but there was little upward pressure on salaries, because there was nothing to buy. Now the shops are full, but any capable person has to have two jobs: one in the old system, and another to make some money. It is illegal, of course, but the 'black economy', which may account for 50% or more of the real economy, has become an essential part of the system, because it is the only way to resolve the absurdities of the official economy.

A foretaste of the competitive threats western companies will be exposed to when the transition is complete, is provided by the changing color of Russian personal computers (PCs). When western embargoes on exports of technology to the Soviet Union were first lifted, the well-educated populations of the Eastern Bears economies were eager to get their hands on these essential tools of modern life. They began importing what they called 'white' computers from American companies, such as IBM or Hewlett-Packard. They took to them like ducks to water and soon demonstrated aptitudes from which a powerful PC software industry will eventually emerge. Russian programmers developed some ten years ago the addictive and ubiquitous PC game Tetrus (or Tetrix), that requires the player to guide configurations of bricks into empty spaces. Soon, Eastern Bears computer buyers realized that much cheaper PCs were available from Taiwan, and the period of the 'yellow' computers began. More recently, the color has changed again and locally made 'red' computers, that sell for a fraction of the cost of 'yellow' computers, are beginning to dominate the market. The Russian PC maker, Vist, makes pretty standard PCs, but all its manuals are printed in Russian, it knows the local market well and has service centers in dozens of Russian cities. It has now become the leading brand in Russia, with a 20% market share.

TOWARDS NORMALIZATION

An analysis of the 1998 installment of the long-running series of Bears' economic and financial crises shows that much of it was of Russia's own making. The costs of servicing its soaring foreign and domestic debt were absorbing a third of its annual budget. Poor tax collection and a soaring budget deficit had added pressure on the ruble, draining Central Bank reserves. An absence of proper bankruptcy laws was keeping many manifestly insolvent enterprises afloat, further reducing the efficiency of the economy. The banks had a lot to answer for, too. Dazzled by the profits available from speculation and investment during the long, global bull market, they had neglected their retail and commercial businesses. Many were insolvent, and only survived because of the inadequate bankruptcy laws. Many foreign companies got badly burned, too, because they had invested too much in fixed assets and not enough in creating a strong local organization, capable of dealing with the recurring problems of any rapidly developing third world country: the Mafia, the political instability, the crazy tax environment.

But in 1998 there were two factors contributing to the crisis over which Russia had no control—the flight of capital from all emerging markets, precipitated by the crisis in Asia, and the subsequent collapse in the world prices of Russia's major export commodities: oil and gas. In the old Soviet siege economy days, the Eastern Bears would not have been exposed to these external shocks, and they have not yet learned how to handle them. Most of their politicians and officials are in their 50s, and have no experience in the management of open economies and societies. They are learning slowly, but the Eastern Bears are unlikely to become 'normal' capitalist countries, until the next generation of politicians brought up on 'glasnost' enters the corridors of power. When thinking about the process of normalization under way in the Eastern Bears, it is helpful to keep in mind the model of economic and social development depicted in Figure 6.8 which is based on an elaboration of work done by Professor Deborah Spar of the Harvard Business School.

The 'political system' sets up domestic and responds to international institutions, such as the Chamber of Commerce, the Central Bank or the International Monetary Fund. These institutions shape the economic environment, by issuing economically significant rules and regulations, such as price and currency controls, but they are in turn shaped by the culture that underpins the political system. In the long run, the economic environment re-shapes the culture, upgrading the political system and the way the market operates. The existing Bears' culture is still shaped by the inefficiencies of central planning and the long-established Russian preference for strong leaders. The Czars had rights of life and death over their people, and successive Communist Party leaders had no hesitation in assuming equivalent power. It seemed natural: Russians

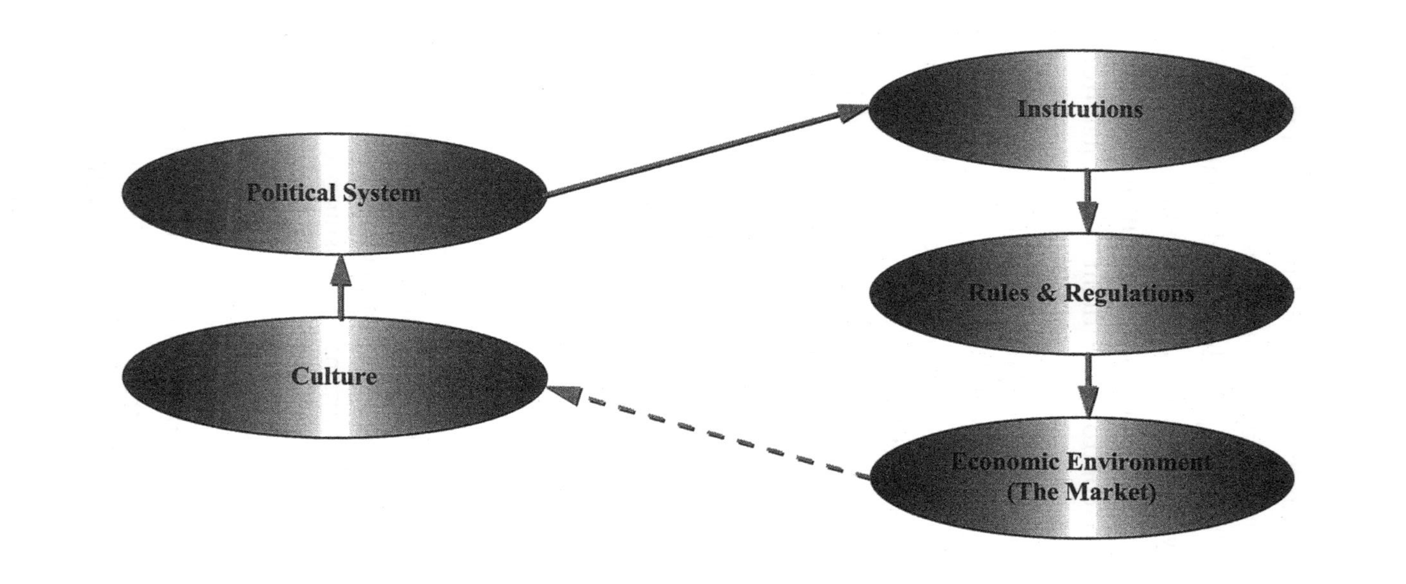

Figure 6.8 How politics affect the market

were used to a very strong 'boss' at the helm of their ship of state. That is why their constitution gives so much power to today's President.

That culture, however, is changing. Educated Russians no longer believe the leader knows best. Before the collapse of the USSR, only 10% of Russians had ever been members of the Communist Party (membership was a great honor and opened the way to power and privilege). Of these, only about 10% had traveled outside the Comecon. That meant that 99% of the people did not know what life was like beyond the barbed wire borders of their closed society, because very effective radio interference had denied them access to western TV. Glasnost, satellite television and a dramatic growth in foreign travel are opening the eyes of working class Russians to western standards of living, and of Russia's emerging middle class to the rich rewards prosperous liberal democracies shower on the most able and well-educated members of their societies. Many Russians over 50 look back with nostalgia to the old system. They were poor and had to wait in line for hours, often in vain, for bare necessities, but their society seemed stable, there was very little crime and everyone had a job. Young Russians expect goods to be in the shops, and know they can vote out of office politicians who fail to meet their expectations. The changing culture makes it very hard to predict the timing of the 'normalization' process, but the genie of liberalism cannot be put back in the bottle. The people of the Eastern Bears have lost their terror of the pogroms and gulags. It would take a river of Russian blood to re-instill the fear and the West would not allow it. Moreover, who would do the killing? Russian soldiers, who refused to fight in Chechnya, are hardly likely to be ready to slaughter their own countrymen in the streets of Moscow.

The transition will not be smooth and there may be periods of right-wing government and illiberal economic policy, but the changing culture is in the driving seat now and there can be no going back. There is a table, in Francis Fukuyama's book *The End of History and the Last Man*, which shows the spread of liberal democracies, worldwide. There were three in 1790: the USA, Switzerland and France. In 1990 there were 61, not including Russia, Belarus or the Ukraine. There is backsliding, from time to time, but it doesn't last and the general direction is clear. The Eastern Bears are on a road that Fukuyama believes all societies must travel.

When contemplating the future that awaits the Eastern Bears, think of Italy, at the end of the Second World War, as it emerged from the fascist dictatorship. It had no natural resources, its illiteracy rate was much higher than Russia's is today, and the Mafia dominated politics in the south. Italy was a real mess in 1948, but five decades later it is the sixth largest economy in the world. How did the Italians do it? Certainly not by having an efficient or stable political system. In 50 years Italy has had over 50 governments, and a mountain of laws and regulations. The Italians became prosperous because they helped themselves, in spite of government intervention and in spite of the Mafia. And so will the Bears, armed with a much higher level of literacy and ample natural resources.

MANAGING THE BEARS

The political and economic volatility that will be a striking feature of the Eastern Bears until they become normalized, means demand trends will be hard to forecast, and companies must remain extremely flexible (see Figure 6.9).

Clearly, importing remains the most flexible way to supply the cluster, but it is also the most expensive way, because import duties, devaluation and transport costs make the goods less attractive in the local market. With the large emerging middle class, small reductions in price have a disproportionate positive effect on volume and market share. Companies should therefore consider local production (requiring major capital investment) or local contract manufacturing. The latter is a very viable alternative, if the right local manufacturer is chosen, and if time and effort is spent in upgrading its quality standards. Another reason why contract manufacturing is an

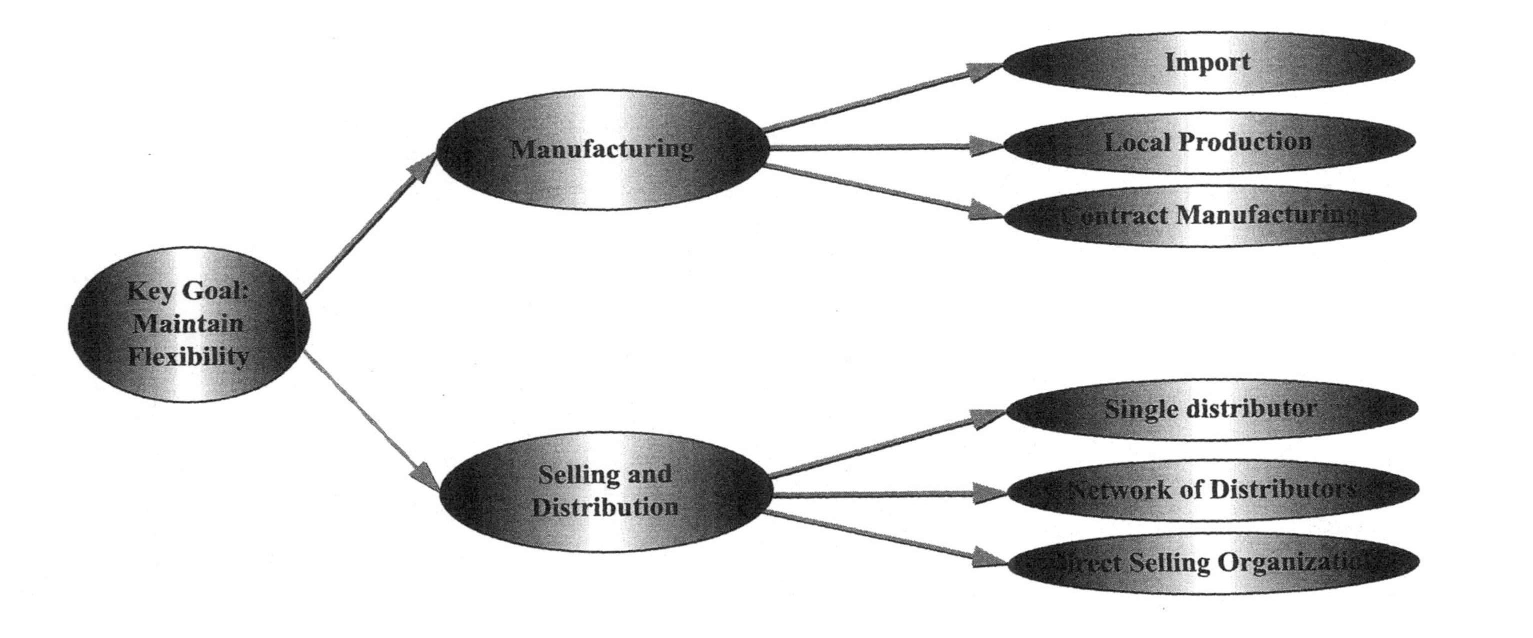

Figure 6.9 Organizational choices

interesting option is that it limits the amount of fixed asset investment sunk in the country. This not only increases the return on capital by reducing the capital base, but also helps maintain a high degree of flexibility when deciding how much volume has to be sold in the market during lean years to maintain a minimum level of profitability.

Likewise in the selling and distributing area. A single distributor is easier to manage, but hard to control. A direct sales force and distribution system is a major investment few companies can afford, especially outside the major cities such as Moscow, St. Petersburg, Kiev and Minsk. Russia is much too large to be considered a single market, and must be broken down into manageable blocks. Of its 150 million population, 25 million live in Moscow and St. Petersburg, 25 million live out in the boon-docks and are virtually unreachable, and the remaining 100 million live in other large cities (see Figure 6.10). Each city needs to be treated as an autonomous area with its own culture and tastes, and is best served by small local distributors. Chapter 7 explains in more detail how to go about establishing such a network. But a word of warning: selling is easy, but collecting accounts receivable is as hard in the Bears as in Latin America. Selling becomes secondary to collecting: a good salesman is one who collects on time what he or she sells.

The two secrets of success in this, the most challenging of all Europe's clusters, are picking manufacturing and distribution partners with care, and constructing an organization capable of succeeding in the most uncertain market conditions, while integrating its operations into a pan-European structure. This is vital. The ruthless Mafia, the inefficient bureaucracy, the illogical taxes, the changing political priorities are second nature to people raised in the Soviet system. Western companies are not investing enough in training these highly capable people to run a subsidiary to western company standards by themselves. (We will return to this issue in Chapter 11.)

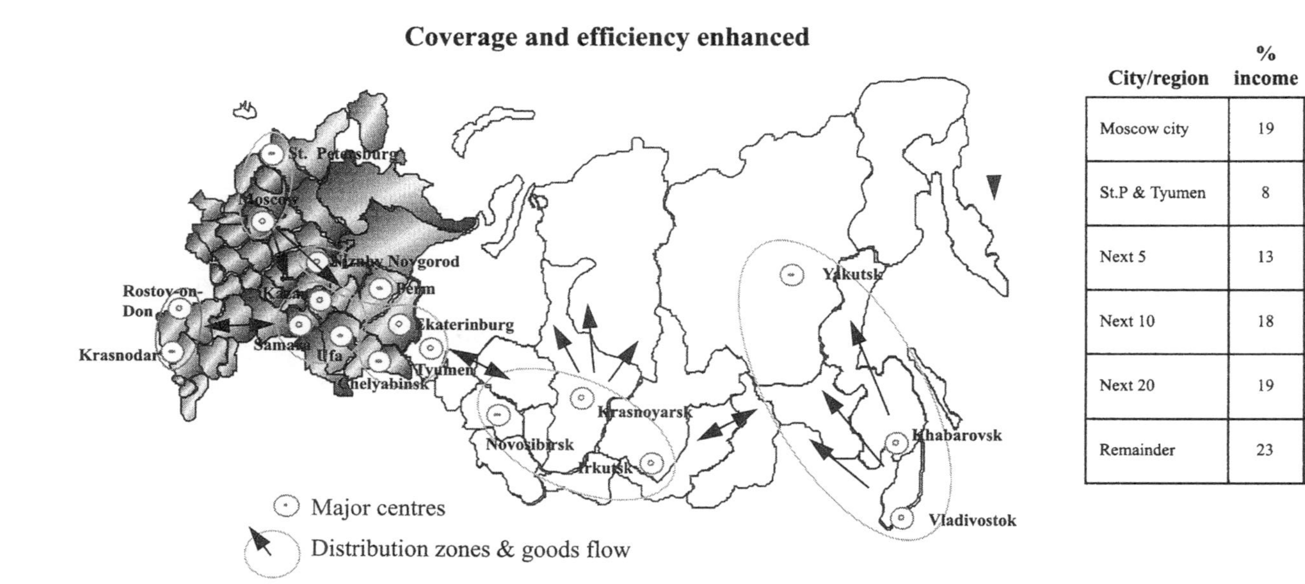

City/region	% income	% pop.
Moscow city	19	6
St.P & Tyumen	8	5
Next 5	13	15
Next 10	18	22
Next 20	19	26
Remainder	23	26

Source: Goskomstat of the Russian Federation – A.T. Kearney elaboration

Figure 6.10 Access and distribution costs in Russia must be controlled by connecting target markets through a network of distribution channels

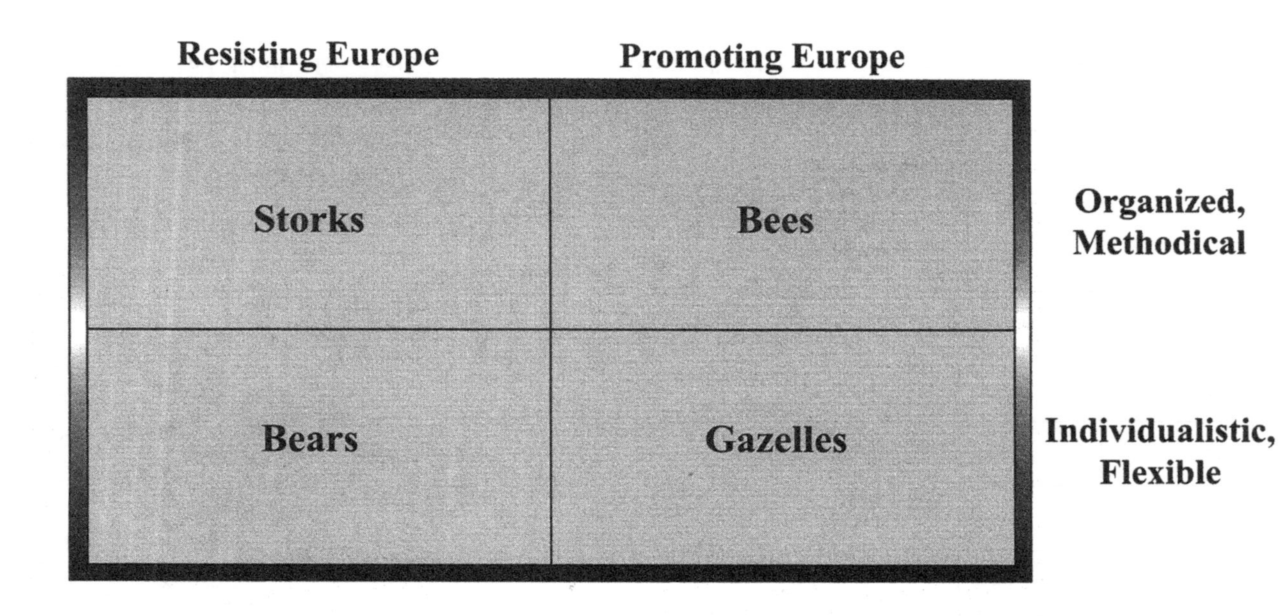

Figure 6.11 Basic cultural differences between clusters

SHARED HERITAGE AND FUTURE, YET DIFFERENT

Just as California 'feels', to a traveler, very different from New England, so it seems safe to assume that, at the end of the 21st century, the Bees will not have become Gazelles, or the Gazelles become Bees. Differences will remain, but not simply north/south divides, as in Italy, or east/west divides, as in Germany. Differences among the clusters are deeper than that. In certain respects, the Bees are like the Gazelles, but in others, they are more like the Storks, and this general mixing of qualities also characterizes the other clusters. Take perceptions of the future, for instance. The Bees and Gazelles want to push for European integration, but the Storks and the Bears remain 'reluctant' Europeans. On the other hand, the flexibility and the strong emphasis on individualism that characterizes both the Gazelles and the Bears, clearly distinguishes them from the methodical, well-organized Bees and Storks. Figure 6.11 helps to visualize these basic cultural differences, which are certain to maintain the multicultural character of this vast continent for decades to come.

Part 2
Managing Greater Europe

7

Organizing for Greater Europe

When looking at greater Europe, the first question a CEO needs to ask himself is: "In which geographical area does my company have the strength and the resources to compete?" In the past, the most favored option, particularly for manufacturers of national niche products (tastes for which vary from country to country), was to operate locally. Food was often cited as a market in which only local brands could compete successfully. This idea of Europe as a collection of discrete markets, separated from one another by national currencies, tariffs, tax regimes and tastes, led to the emergence of a standard European organizational model, of the kind shown in Figure 7.1. The headquarters was small, and acted as the manager of a portfolio of country operations, with broad supervisory, financial control and consolidation roles. Everything else, from research and development (R&D) to human resources (HR), was done by autonomous national operating companies under strict instructions not to compete with each other by exporting products to neighboring countries.

The model worked well enough while those differences between countries that had inspired it remained, but now that a single currency is used within most of Europe and all tariffs with eastern Europe are being reduced, it is becoming increasingly outdated. From a business point of view it is clear that greater Europe is becoming an integrated market, while retaining its precious cultural pluralism. The growth, in recent years, of parallel imports, made possible by the dismantling of tariff barriers, is not only a serious threat to the integrity of the old organizational model; it is also a reflection of a steady convergence of European appetites. Even in foods, markets for national niche products are blurring together as tastes diffuse and demand for 'ethnic' products migrates across borders. Twenty years ago demand for pasta 'al dente' was confined to Italy. Today, it is available in good restaurants all over Europe, while breakfast cereals and hamburgers unknown in Italy two decades ago, have since become popular with Italian youngsters.

In some respects, the gradual blurring of national niche markets is a curse for manufacturers, because it robs them of the freedom they enjoyed previously to vary their prices from country to country. In other respects, however, it is a blessing, because it offers an opportunity to capture extra economies of scale, at a time when their small local brands are coming under vigorous attack by retailers' private-labels.

THE THREAT OF PRIVATE-LABELS

For companies that plan to operate only locally, the sternest competition will come from their own clients. In Europe, the growth of 'private-labels' is transforming retailers from customers of manufacturers to powerful competitors with a trump card—an intimate knowledge of the plan for new products, marketing, advertising and promotion for the branded goods they compete with. There's nothing new about retailers' labels, but in the highly concentrated European supermarket industry where just a few major chains dominate each national market, they seem particularly threatening, because retailers have proved very adept at developing their own brand equity. In the UK, for example, the top five supermarket chains account for two-thirds of the total grocery market (see Figure 7.2) and private-label business in packaged groceries has grown in three years from around 34% to almost 40% of supermarket sales. At Sainsbury's, own-labels account for two-thirds of all sales.

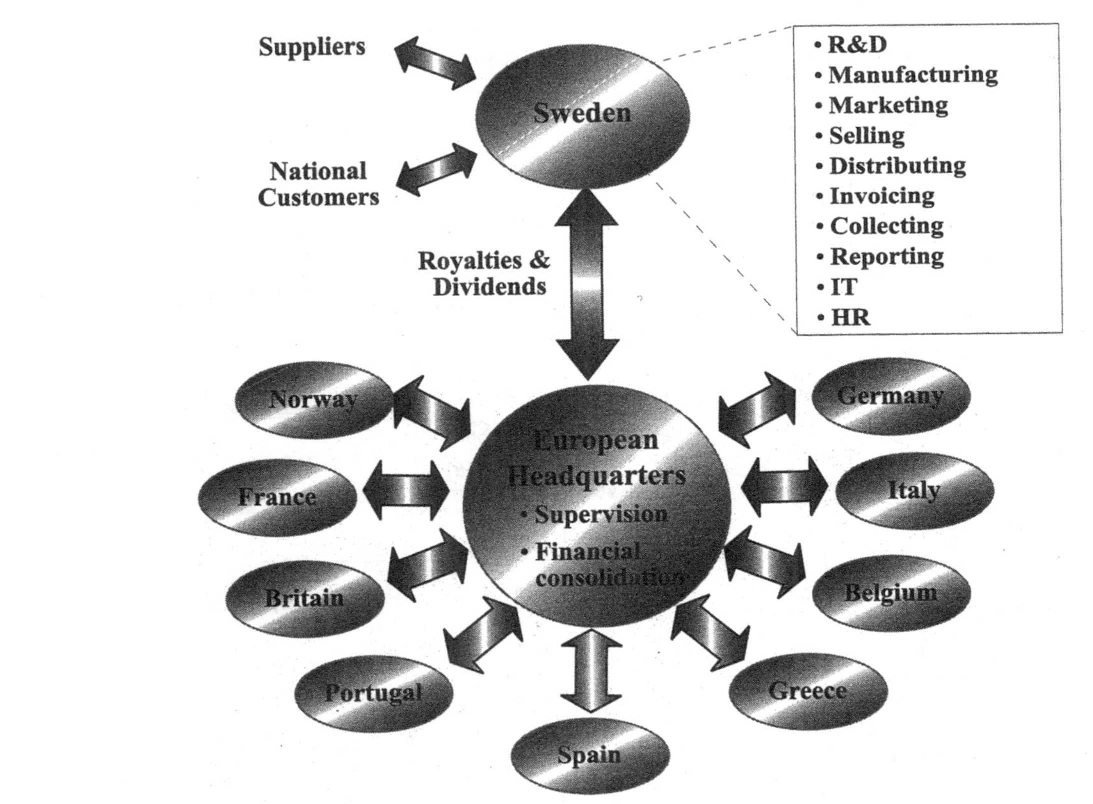

Figure 7.1 Standard European organizational model

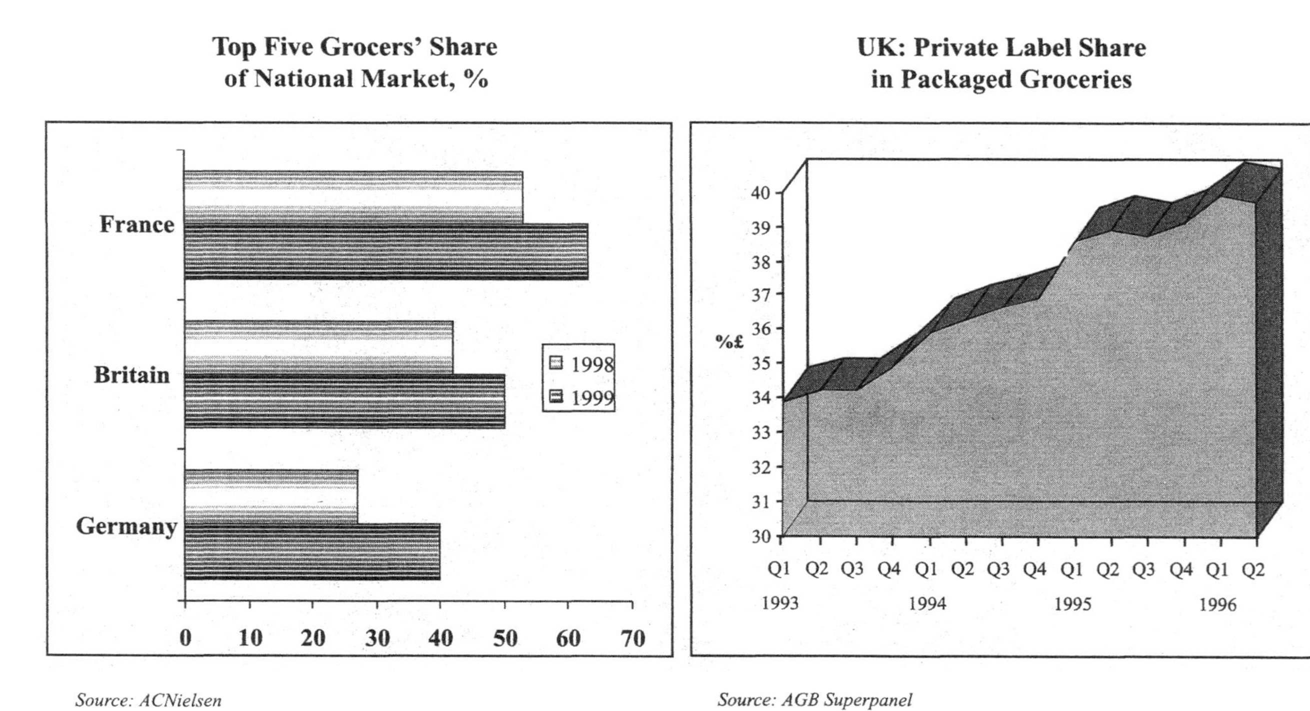

Figure 7.2 Market shares of supermarkets and private labels

Some of Europe's major grocery chains are now expanding into eastern Europe (the UK's Tesco, for example, already has 48 stores in Hungary alone), and once established, are sure to play the private-label card in these markets, too. Moreover, as the quality of own-label goods improves, manufacturers of branded goods are coming under increasing pressure to compete on price at a time when the euro is greatly expanding the bargain-hunting horizons of Europe's increasingly price-sensitive consumers.

What, if anything, can manufacturers do about the private-label threat? The fundamental, strategic decision for manufacturers is whether or not to manufacture 'own-label' products for trade customers. Some manufacturers—including such heavyweights as Kraft Jacobs Suchard and Heinz—have chosen to bite this particular bullet and undertake private-label contract work. It helps to absorb their spare plant capacity, allows them to reap extra economies of scale in manufacturing and purchasing, and liberates resources that can be devoted to strengthening key brands. Others, including Kellogg and Procter & Gamble, have declined to drink from what they see as the poisoned chalice of private-label manufacturing, for fear that it will undermine their competitive position and seriously damage their brand equity. For their part, the major retailers see the private-label business as a way to differentiate themselves from competitors, as a profit opportunity, and as a way to generate additional returns from advertising invested in the brand equity of their store chains. (Sometimes, they exaggerate the profitability of their private-labels, by not allocating costs properly. When Sainsbury's launched its Novon private-label detergent, it raided corporate advertising budgets to promote it. If this advertising had been properly allocated to the private-label profit and loss account, Novon's profitability would have been seen to be considerably lower than reported.)

The growing intensity of the new rivalry between private-labels and branded goods is illustrated by the proliferation of 'lookalikes', which mimic the key identification traits of the brand, sometimes giving the impression to consumers that the private-label is made by the manufacturer of the copied brand. Kellogg is well known to have suffered from this misperception. A UK survey found that one in five consumers had bought lookalikes, because they thought they were made by the manufacturer of the brand they resembled. According to the European Brands Association, AIM, lookalikes are seen as a significant problem in nine European countries, with 412 incidents reported over a four year period.

Manufacturers that decide to take on the private-label business, should regularly re-assess its profitability and be sure to allocate overheads properly to their private-label operations. Pricing should also be regularly monitored. In the early days of a contract manufacturing relationship, the retailer tends to see quality and service as the priorities. Later on, when the quality and service offered by other manufacturers has improved, questions of price tend to loom larger. When a major retailing client threatens to de-list both the brand and the private-label if the manufacturer refuses to agree to a lower price, one realizes why some manufacturers regard the own-label business as a poisoned chalice. More than one major manufacturer has undertaken private-label work, only to regret it later, and pull out.

In the fight with this tough local competitor, all companies must remember that all products must offer the consumer good value for money. When Philip Morris cut the price of Marlboro cigarettes by 25% in an attempt to regain market share from private-labels, its stock price plummeted. Subsequent reports that this heralded 'the death of brands' proved premature, however. Marlboro sales more than recovered as perceptions of the brand's value for money rose again relative to competing products. Frequent promotions can give the impression that the product is over-priced when not being promoted, but careful design of in-store promotions can make it harder for retailers to use 'compare and save' tactics effectively. Using proprietary packaging, and resisting the temptation to use standard containers also available to private-labels, can help deter imitators, but it is also important to be proactive about lookalikes by consulting trademark advisers at an early stage in the packaging design process. Registration across the EU is now possible not only for the trademark, but also for distinctive pack or label designs. Money invested in a consistently aggressive legal response to imitators, is money well spent on preserving brand equity.

It is also useful to explore alternative marketing and distribution channels. Retailers, such as Tesco in the UK, are experimenting with new channels such as home delivery, but there is no reason why manufacturers should not follow suit. In the USA, Mars is offering quality chocolates through a web-site, delivered by Federal Express. In Switzerland, Nestlé is testing a tele-sales service called 'Easy Shop' with 800 households, using a TV set, and a control box the size of a video cassette recorder.

Even European manufacturers that plan to compete in a whole cluster or in several clusters are right to be worried about 'private-labels', but they are not quite as over-matched in their struggle for trade margin as companies that plan to operate in a single country. A comprehensive strategy for private-labels, of the kind outlined above is vital, but the most important move a branded goods manufacturer can make in its struggle with retailers and other rivals is to redesign its organization.

EFFICIENCY IS THE BEST POLICY

The great weakness of the traditional organizational model shown on Figure 7.1 is that it prevents companies from exploiting their greater ability to innovate (their most important advantage in their struggle with retailers), and does not allow them to realize the new economies of scale, created by the integration of the European market. Companies operating across borders need to re-configure their internal value chains, so they can be local where being local creates value, and European where being European improves efficiency. Capturing continental economies of scale in R&D, manufacturing, 'sourcing' and distribution (see Chapters 8–10) frees

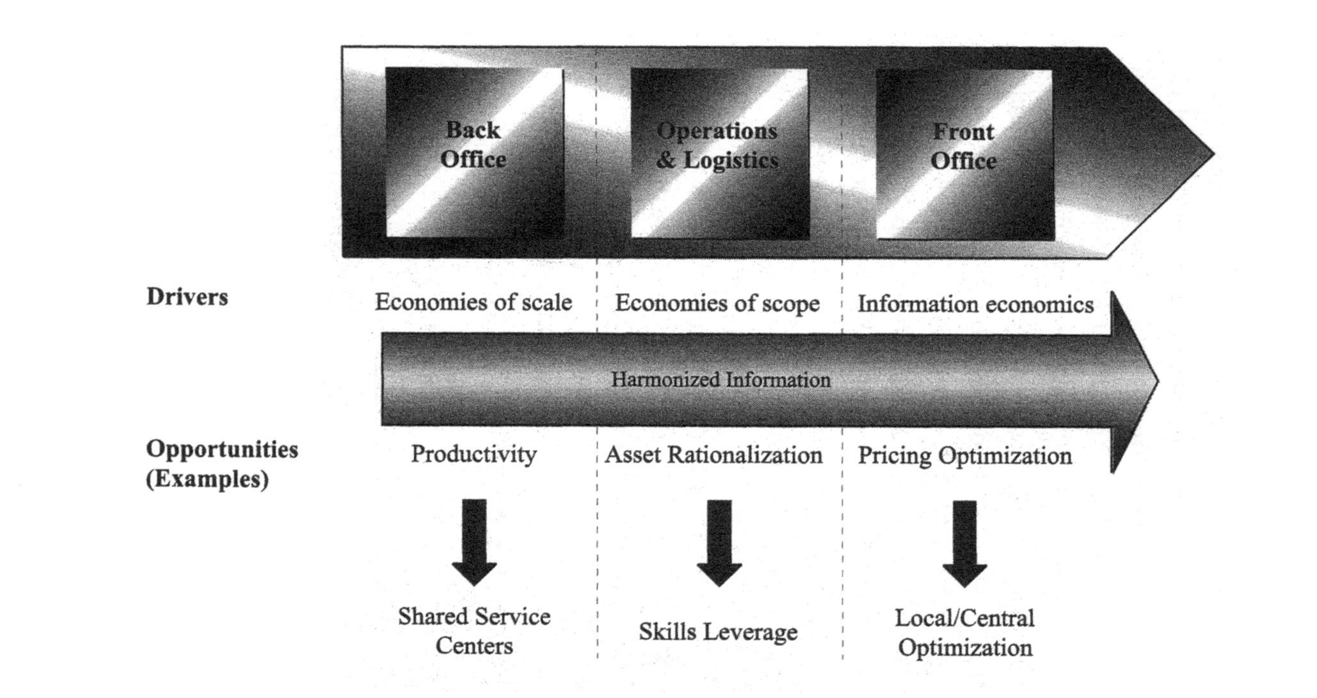

Figure 7.3 Back office and supply chain consolidation offers broader benefits which should be exploited early to increase operations efficiency and front office effectiveness

resources for investing in brand equity through product innovation, and extra consumer advertising and trial generating promotions.

Figure 7.3 locates the new economies offered by the integration of the European market on the internal value chain, and indicates the order in which efforts should be made to capture them. Front offices must remain local of course, and re-organizations elsewhere must strengthen their local competitiveness. Ideally, a customer or a consumer should not even know that the company has re-organized. They are still serviced by the same friendly salesman or consumer response center. But capturing economies of scale in back offices, and economies of scope in operations and logistics, can put powerful weapons in the hands of front offices, in their struggles with local private-labels. Although a Sainsbury's private-label may command a majority of its category's sales in Sainsbury's supermarkets, its share of the UK market is less than 10% and its share of the greater European market (including eastern Europe) is just a fraction of 1%. Since retailer brands do not travel as easily or as quickly as product brands, Europe's enlargement offers manufacturers an opportunity to capture much greater economies of scale than those available to retailers.

According to Antony Burgmans, Chairman of Unilever, the eventual outcome of the war of attrition between brands and own-labels, will be the elimination of minor brands. He predicts that the top two or three places in each category will be claimed by major brands, often pan-European or global, and private-labels will replace the rest. If he's right, manufacturers must select their champion brands very carefully, 'support strength' as von Clausewitz urged, with innovative products and creative marketing, and adopt new organizational designs more suited to the larger and more integrated European market.

The general shape of the new model generated by the value chain perspective is shown on Figure 7.4. In this model, the center (which can have a number of physical locations) controls the value-added chain. Factories are paid a transformation fee (similar to that paid

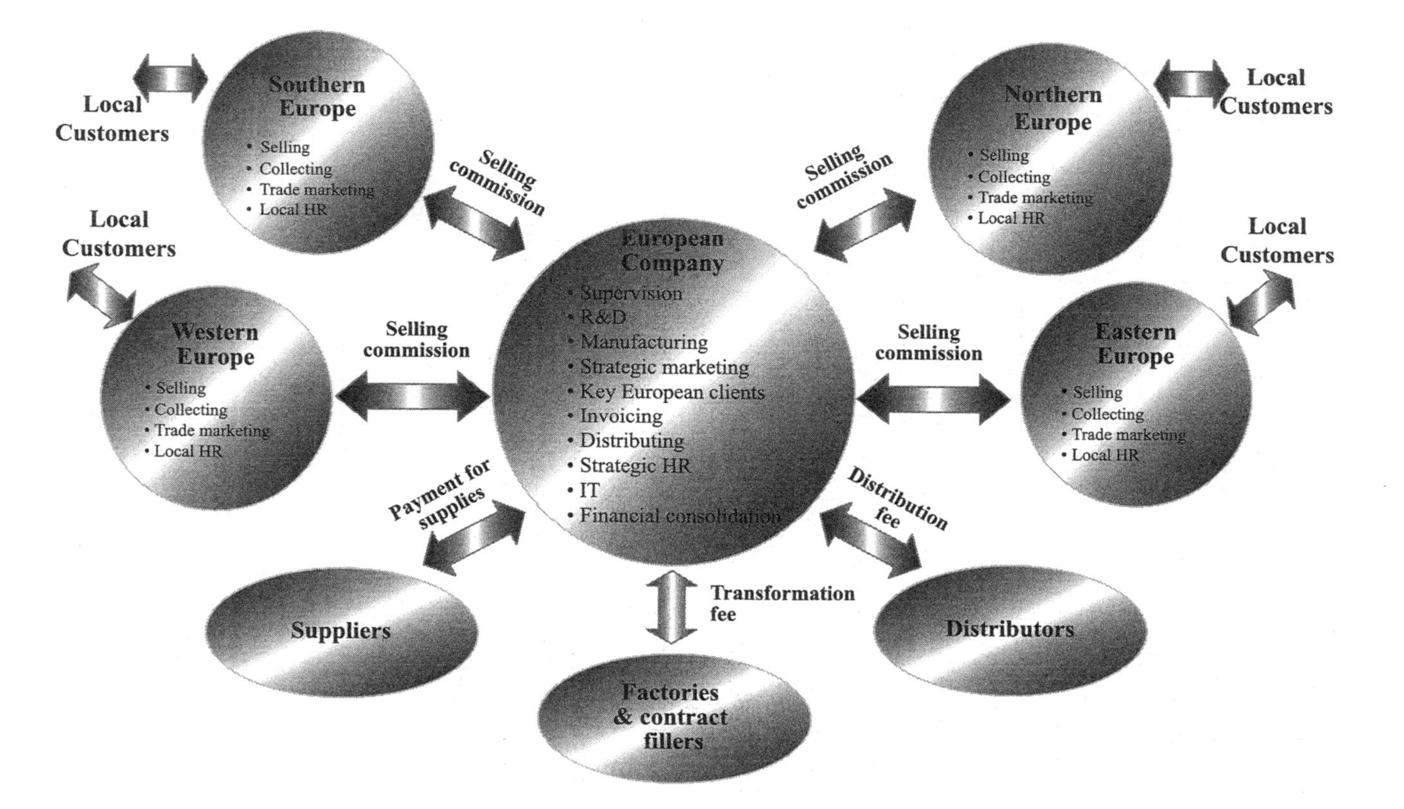

Figure 7.4 New model

to contract manufacturers), while front offices are paid a 'selling and collecting' fee, like sales agents. Invoicing is centralized, and so is the payment of suppliers and deliveries to clients. The next four chapters will be devoted to exploring the new model's merits and the implications for innovation, marketing, the supply chain and the back office.

Before considering these vital operational issues, however, we will look at one of the model's most significant virtues in modern Europe—the relative ease with which it allows the addition of new territories to the geographical portfolio. This is where the 'cluster' model described in Part 1, is united with the organizational model we will be exploring in Part 2.

ENTERING NEW MARKETS

Under the old scheme, a new country in a geographical portfolio usually required a disproportionate amount of investment, training and supervision to set up an infrastructure capable of manufacturing, billing, delivering and innovating. This is particularly true of eastern European countries, many of which remain burdened by archaic and conflicting laws, regulations and practices. The new organizational model does not generate unique answers to all of the questions raised by a decision to expand into new markets, but it provides a framework within which they can be addressed. It is much more flexible, in the sense that it offers many more options, than the traditional model. To open a new country, all one needs to do is to establish an efficient front office, and develop an effective distribution system.

The first question that needs to be answered when contemplating entry into a new market, is whether customers and consumers should be approached through a distributor or a representative office, with a joint venture or a wholly-owned subsidiary or with a planned progression from one to the other. Because the new model does not favor a particular approach, it allows the choice to be based on a thorough analysis, that attaches priorities to eastern European markets on the basis of potential demand and rates of deregulation (see Chapter 2). A low priority country is best approached through one carefully monitored distributor, but for a rapidly deregulating or large country, a good low-cost half-way house is a representative office, managing a number of distributor relationships. US spice maker, McCormick, entered Russia a few years ago through one local distributor controlled by its Finnish subsidiary. Russia then became its fastest growing market in Europe—sales doubled within two years. But if this growth is to be maintained, how long can McCormick continue serving its Russian customers well through a single distributor? Distributors tend to be undercapitalized, and ill equipped to cope with rapid sales growth, so growth increases the chances of payment delays, and even default. Before it gets to that, distributors need to be replaced by a network of distributors co-ordinated by a new representative office, or by a sales subsidiary.

Another important question is whether or not to establish a tax base in the new country. This will trigger a substantial increase in overheads, because a tax base will require compliance with complex tax reporting requirements. However, establishing a wholly-owned subsidiary, either through a greenfield start-up or an acquisition, may be desirable in a high priority country, because it allows the entrant to take a more aggressive approach to the market. It costs more than importing through distributors, it is riskier, and brings with it a host of further complications, such as the need to recruit management and staff, so the potential of the market must be substantial to make such a commitment worthwhile.

Another option for the new entrant is to form a joint venture with a local company. This helps to reduce cost and risk and, in certain countries, such as Russia, has the important advantage of providing a ready-made network of local contacts for negotiating with officials. It might also provide access to an established distribution network, and in any event, it eliminates one potential competitor. The main drawbacks are the invariably underestimated problems of achieving a mutually beneficial 'modus operandi', with partners who are unused to western business practices, priorities and communications styles. Moreover, corporate priorities change and a joint venture that began with a perfectly aligned set of goals, may become strained over time as unforeseen developments cause partners' interests to diverge. It's wise, therefore, to agree termination clauses at the outset, when goodwill among partners is at its highest.

The type of market presence chosen will, in turn, determine how the country reports back through the organization. The secret here is to integrate the new markets into the existing organizational structure without adding extra management layers. This is no easy task of course, but a number of pitfalls can be avoided if you keep Europe together. It is generally better to have eastern Europe report directly to the CEO of western Europe, than to the vice president of international operations. In the Northern Bees, eastern European markets are integrating so rapidly with western European markets that separating them can cause communications problems and reduce responsiveness. At one major toiletries manufacturer, eastern Europe initially reported through International, to the US corporate headquarters, rather than the western European organization. Communications lines became unduly lengthy when, for instance, briefing the Polish operations about the rapid expansion of German retailers

While markets remain small and economically undeveloped, eastern Europe may report to the European CEO via a director of eastern Europe. As these economies (and the company's business with them) expand, develop and become increasingly integrated with the western European and world economies, CEOs should 'cluster' them with major western economies, as proposed in Part 1. Quest International is one of the three largest European manufacturers of industrial perfumes. In recent years, it has opened offices in Moscow, Kiev, Prague and Warsaw, and has chosen to manage all of them from Germany where it has the resources to provide the support some of its clients need in eastern Europe.

This approach does not require the creation of additional management layers and encourages the capture of synergies, such as multilanguage labeling and common 'cluster' promotions to retailers, thus helping to prepare for closer integration in the future. It also minimizes the number of reports to the European CEO while exploiting the skills and expanding the responsibilities of major country managers. When well executed, such 'clustering' within the new organizational model shown on Figure 7.4, can help companies capture a number of other economies and 'synergies' we shall explore in the next four chapters.

MORE CENTRALIZED AND MORE LOCALIZED

It will not have escaped the reader's notice that the model of organization proposed here is much more centralized than the traditional model (shown on Figure 7.1). The responsibilities of the managers of the clusters are confined to 'front office' operations—selling, collecting, and local marketing and HR. At a time when business unit autonomy is widely seen as an essential pre-requisite for corporate flexibility, the new model may appear to be excessively centralized. But such centralization is the only way manufacturers can capture the scale economies offered by greater Europe, and which they need so desperately, in their power struggles with retailers. Moreover, the centralization does not reduce 'local' flexibility significantly. On the contrary, by centralizing back office and operating functions, it allows the cluster front offices to concentrate all their attention on getting close to their customers and consumers.

As we have seen, the new model makes the company more agile in terms of its speed of entering new markets, because it doesn't have to establish new, fully functional operations in each new country—it simply has to set up a viable front office and distribution system. There are tax planning benefits too. Following the resignation of Germany's finance minister, Oskar Lafontaine in 1999, there seems little chance that his vision of a tax-harmonized

EU will be realized in the foreseeable future. While corporate tax rates vary, an organizational model that allows a central invoicing center to be located in the country where tax rates are lowest is an obvious advantage.

The relationship between flexibility and structure is not a simple one. The challenge, in Europe and elsewhere, is to make local operations as flexible as possible, make the whole organization as efficient as possible, and make sure that the interfaces between the center, on the one hand, and the local operations, suppliers, distributors and sub-contractors, on the other, work smoothly.

8
The Innovation Imperative

According to Peter Brabeck-Letmathe of Nestlé: 'to develop fully a leading edge business segment today, a company must be prepared to invest heavily in R&D—in the range of €500 million to €1 billion.' At those spending levels, companies have no choice but to focus on their core competencies and leverage economies of scale by centralizing R&D as much as possible. This is, of course, a global, not just a European requirement, but organizing for successful innovation in Europe requires substantial re-adjustments, because, as we have seen, R&D has traditionally been assigned to local subsidiaries. It must be centralized, because local subsidiaries lack the economies of scale needed for technological breakthroughs, but the consolidation process needs to be handled with great care.

Companies are right to be concerned that such centralized R&D departments, remote from customers, will develop new products that local markets don't want, or will fail to build in local adaptations early enough. Local variants are often crucial to success, especially in food. But developing products suitable for only one or two European countries, as even some multinational companies continue to do, spreads R&D efforts over hundreds of projects, none of which produce any technological superiority and the new features of which are easily copied by private-labels. In their anxiety to remain locally sensitive, these companies go too far the other way and rely on local R&D units that are too small to attract the caliber of researchers or to command the financial resources needed to develop superior products. The dilemma is, in a sense, resolving itself in that patterns of innovation are evolving to a point where responsiveness to consumers is ceasing to be the secret of success.

BREAKING THE CONSUMER-DRIVEN PARADIGM

A number of CEOs are becoming convinced that to be a leader in innovation today, the old paradigm of the 'consumer-driven company' must be abandoned. According to Jacques Vincent of Danone: "It's not enough any longer to canvass consumers, to find out what they want. In the increasingly competitive western world, companies must anticipate consumer trends, and then convince those consumers of the new values that innovation brings to them."

Leading-edge companies are relying much less on local demands to drive their R&D, and are endeavoring, instead, to develop central strategies that seek technological advantage in areas of their core competence, to meet emerging needs that may not yet be apparent at the local level. Nowhere does this approach have greater potential for reaping synergies than in Europe. As the euro develops as the single currency, and as candidate EU members like Poland continue to align their regulations with those of the EU in anticipation of being admitted, a new pan-European market is emerging with a growing hunger for pan-European products. The market-integrating effects of regulatory convergence, and single currency help to explain why a study conducted by A.T. Kearney suggests that companies that 'over-globalize' tend to out-perform those that 'over-localize' (see Figure 8.1).

BUILDING IN LOCAL FLEXIBILITY

Since local differences in tastes will remain for many years to come, it is essential that the centralized R&D organization should remain open to timely local input. Such flexibility can be built in, by following a few simple guidelines.

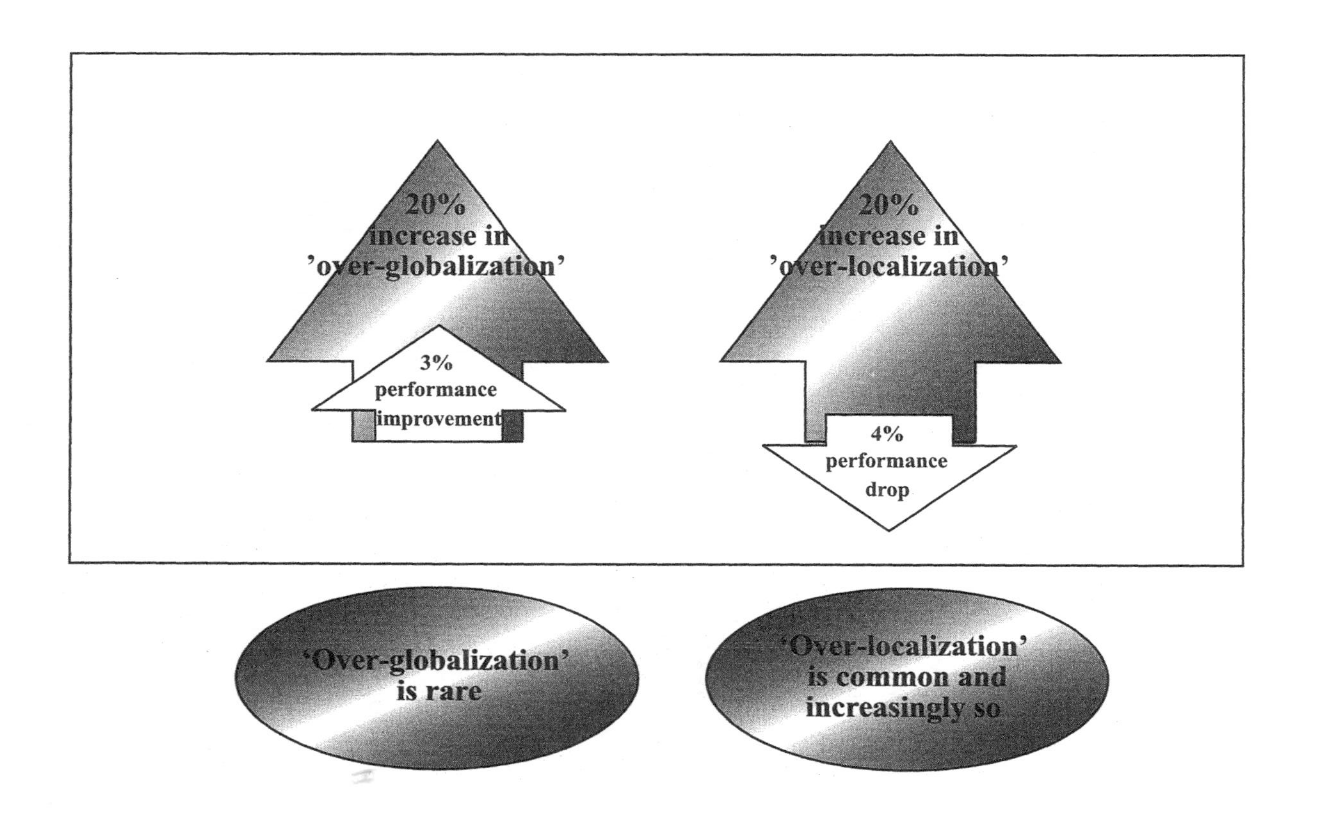

Figure 8.1 It is better to be 'too global' than 'too local'

Create a strong R&D center. The question of where it should be located is best determined by the locations of 'centers of expertise' which are becoming increasingly well defined in Europe. At Unilever, for example, Paris is being developed as a center of excellence for hair care, and Rome has become the center of excellence for developing adult ice cream. It is vital, however, that the R&D center can communicate easily with the European universities that are most advanced in the technology of interest to the company. And too few companies are yet taking advantage of the excellent value-for-money offered by the well-qualified, low-cost scientists of the Eastern Bear cluster.

Establish a strategic direction. This should be done by the relevant 'strategic business unit' (SBU). R&D staff cannot deal directly with the large number of requests from local markets and nor should they, but local expertise must be sought frequently and sufficiently early on in the R&D process, to ensure efficient local customization, where necessary. This requires some kind of central marketing interface, to align R&D with the company's strategic goals, and to co-ordinate demands from local markets for innovations or for customization of R&D in progress. One person may fill this important central role—say a European Brand Manager—or a team. A broad range of skills is needed, from business development to marketing, and so is a good understanding of trade and consumer needs in the major markets and a direct line to top management. Such interfaces tend to be most effective when located near the R&D center.

At Nestlé, SBUs identify the categories where innovation is needed, R&D is then undertaken at one of a number of centers around the world, and the new product that emerges is adapted to local tastes by country teams. Nestlé's LC1 product, a yogurt containing active bacteria which help to sustain the body's natural defenses, emerged from a process that began when a foods SBU identified 'healthy foods' as a key category for innovation.

Create virtual teams. Good active links between the R&D center, the markets and the central interface are crucial, and can be achieved simply and cheaply with e-mail, voicemail and video conferencing modules that can be added to a PC for around €1,000.

Reduce time to market. The need for local adaptations tends to inhibit rapid Europe-wide rollout, but times to market can be minimized, if the center always keeps local markets up to date with progress in the development process. Forewarned and fully briefed local organizations can alert the trade, develop promotional material and prepare the consumer.

Consider market priorities when planning local adaptations. This will help to minimize the costs of customization, and so maximize economies of scale. For instance, a company might decide to customize for Russia and France, but not Hungary or Belgium. Or it may decide not to customize at all for markets at an early stage of development. Such decisions should be made at the center. A possibility offered by our new model is to customize by cluster—to customize for the Northern Bees, for example, by taking into account German consumer and trade needs, but not those of countries clustered to it, such as Switzerland, Austria, and the Scandinavian countries. As we have seen, members of a properly assembled cluster are converging on one another culturally, and economically, and are thus constantly producing new opportunities to capture synergies. It is essential to ensure all costs are considered, when assessing the costs and benefits of further customization, such as the cost of the extra inventory, and the cost of the increased complexity for manufacturing and the distribution network. Often these complexity costs are underestimated, resulting in a less than optimal cost structure for the whole company.

A TWO-PRONGED INNOVATION STRATEGY

When developing an innovation strategy, it is also essential to take into account the differences in the sophistication of markets within clusters. Such differences are so important in greater Europe, that a strong case can be made for developing two separate strands in an innovation strategy.

For the Eastern Bears and the eastern European markets of the Southern Gazelles, where penetration is very low, price is crucial to build sales volumes. For these markets, simple, 'no-frills' products, offering western quality at low prices, are most likely to increase penetration quickly, and establish firm footholds. Five years ago, most Russians used soap, ash, soda and hot water for dishwashing. What they needed was a basic dishwashing detergent—Procter & Gamble's new, high-tech 'anti-bacterial' dishwasher liquid would have been far too sophisticated and expensive for them.

On the other hand, in western Europe, where demand is flat and product penetration is high, innovation efforts should be devoted to developing more sophisticated product variants, to increase the value of each purchase. Manufacturers should endeavor to maintain the perceived product value at a higher price by adding benefits. Gillette dominated western Europe's 'wet shaving' market with single- and double-blade shavers and would have been a long way down the diminishing returns curve, if it had tried to increase its market share. However, its three-blade razor has an additional benefit (that extra blade), so it can command a higher price. The margin may be unchanged in percentage terms, but is higher in absolute terms.

The differences between these two 'innovation strategies' and their products raises the issue of brands. A case for uniform pan-European brands will be made in the next chapter, but an intermediate brand strategy is needed to cover the process of east/west economic integration. Brands come in families, and each family member matures, over time. A marketer's perspective on the 'two-pronged innovation strategy' proposed above, might be that eastern European markets require 'immature' brands, that is western European brands taken back to their original forms. The beauty of it is that they can be sold at lower prices, because, thanks to new technology, they can be manufactured more cheaply now. But the brand footprints they establish must prepare the way for the introduction of more 'mature', higher-priced variants as disposable incomes in eastern Europe rise. In other words, when devising the entry brand, clever marketers already have in mind a brand migration or upgrade path (see Chapter 9). The important point is that the low-cost entry brand designed for fast penetration must be endowed, at the outset, with the potential to spawn higher-priced more sophisticated successor brands, of the kind that will be in demand five, and then ten years after market entry.

A centralized R&D program can accommodate a dual innovation strategy of this kind, and need not be seen as favoring the pursuit of economies of scale, at the expense of local responsiveness. On the contrary, it can stimulate significant (as opposed to trivial, easily copied) innovation, and anticipate local needs at the same time.

PROTECTING INNOVATION

Significant innovation is crucial, because the private-labels are making it increasingly hard to win market share by clever market positioning, and because innovations that are easy to copy, technically and legally, confer no advantage. Lawyers should, therefore, be brought in at an early stage, to assess what can be protected by patent, trademark or copyright. Some say patents in the consumer goods industry are not worth the paper they're written on, and that it is better to try to keep ahead of one's competitors, by innovating more quickly and more frequently. The problem with this approach is that it does not take into account today's reality: the development of private-labels has dramatically reduced the 'copy' time of a competitor. Now that a 'lookalike' can be ready to ambush a new product within weeks of launch, manufacturers should spend more resources and time to protect the fruits of their R&D labors.

The broader the area of protection, the better and, generally speaking, a product patent provides broader protection than a process patent. Unilever has patented a toilet block with bleach.

That prevents anyone from producing the product, even those who work out a way to do it using a process different from the one used by Unilever. The wider the geographical area of protection the better, too. Pan-European protection, by which all new EU members will be bound on entry (and aspiring new entrants may thus deem it prudent to comply with, prior to entry) is now available from the European patent office in Spain. An advantage of an active patent protection policy is that it sends a strong signal to would-be copiers. Market signaling is very useful in this politically delicate area. For example, the money Nescafé invested in advertising its new-shape container puzzled some people. Others read the campaign as a message to those tempted to copy it, that Nestlé regarded the new shape as commercially valuable. Moreover, Nestlé would have no trouble in demonstrating substantial damage (in the form of the money it had spent on advertising its launch), if it brought a case against a look-alike container. The dilemma, as all consumer goods manufacturers are only too well aware, is that seeking legal redress against the private-label copy, may provoke the retailer defendant into de-listing the original product.

This is a major problem for the consumer goods value chain. A high rate of innovation is obviously in the interests of the whole value chain, including retailers, but the manufacturers will be reluctant to make the necessary investments, if their trade customers routinely use the threat of de-listing to take a free, private-label ride on every new product.

9
Brands, Prices and the Euro

As companies expand across Europe by acquiring other companies, they are collecting brands and trademarks by the dozen. That is often the object of such exercises: those acquired brands may bolster a company's market share, provide an entry into a strategic product category, or just eliminate a competitor. But acquisitive companies often fail to deal effectively with the consequences. As a company's brands proliferate, they may start to cannibalize each other and the cost of complexity in manufacturing, sales and distribution inevitably rises. So do the costs of advertising and R&D, because the more the brands, the higher the advertising spend needed to make an impact and the greater the need for innovation. Moreover, there is some evidence that consumers are beginning to balk at the bewildering array of choices for each product. In frozen confectionery, for instance, nearly 1,200 different lines are available in UK grocery stores, 31% more than the 900-odd two years previously (see Figure 9.1). Some brand manufacturers, such as Procter & Gamble, have increased their shares in several categories by cutting product lines, and eliminating minor brands.

Those who fail to tackle the challenge of rationalizing their huge brand portfolios in Europe's increasingly competitive markets are likely to fall behind. Many are reluctant to do so, because they see multiple brands as a defense against the attacks of own-label goods, which are often their toughest local competitors. However, in the battle with own-labels multiple brands are a weakness, not a strength.

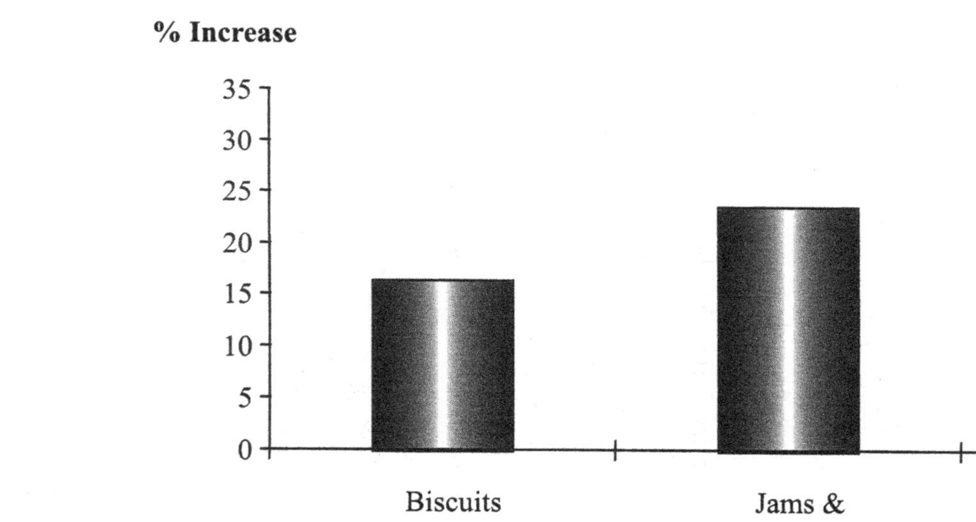

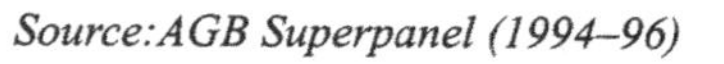

Source:AGB Superpanel (1994–96)

Figure 9.1 Proliferation of brands and lines in all UK retail outlets

The local own-label threat can best be met by developing single European, or global brands, and capturing economies of scale that are beyond the reach of most national retailing chains.

POTENTIAL ECONOMIES

The main savings from strong, pan-European brands come in the form of advertising costs which typically range from 5 to 15% of a product's sales. This can be reduced significantly with pan-European advertising, through trans-national media. Some 80% of Swiss households, for example, regularly watch German TV, and, more significantly, cable and satellite broadcasters are rapidly expanding their coverage. The Eurosport channel now reaches nearly 40% of western European households (see Figure 9.2), and CNN and MTV reach definable market segments, worldwide. Chris Ingram, chairman of Tempus Group—one of Europe's largest media buyers—warns that the coverage of cable and satellite TV has been growing so fast, that "pan-European companies that continue to ignore these cost-effective media risk leaving themselves open to competition."

The growing acceptance of multilingual labels by industry and consumers alike, creates potential savings in packaging and labeling and in the case of brands that do not require local variations in flavor, fragrance or appearance, this reduces manufacturing complexity, and inventory. Furthermore, uniform brands with multilingual labels, are easy to ship to wherever they are needed, enabling companies to reduce inventories and improve consumer responsiveness at the same time. Finally, strong Euro-brands can give manufacturers bargaining leverage with trade customers that are also expanding across Europe, such as Auchan, Carrefour, Metro, Promodes, Rewe, and Tesco.

BRAND MIGRATION

As awareness of the value of brand equity has grown, managers have become increasingly reluctant to change brands, and most brand managers are anxious to discourage any such suggestion.

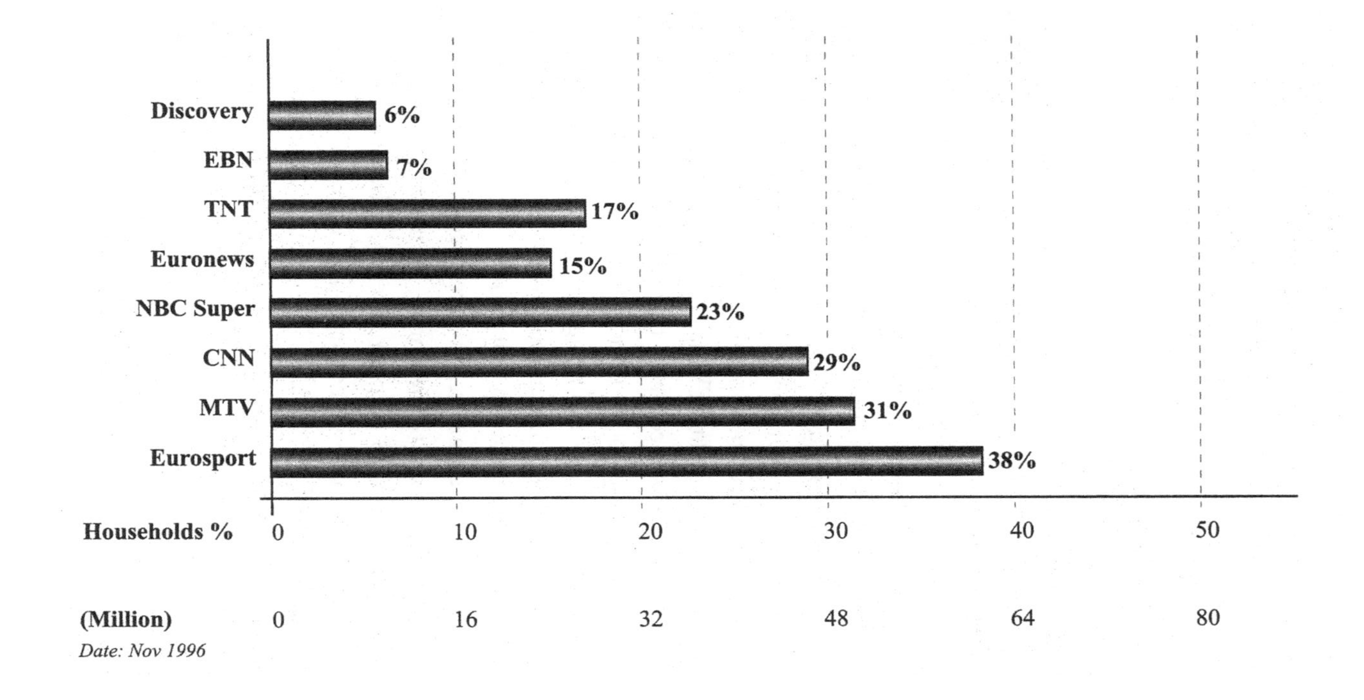

Figure 9.2 Home penetration in key European markets

When Mars changed the name of its popular Marathon bar in the UK to Snickers—the name used in the rest of the world—it did so overnight. This 'cold turkey' approach may seem risky and expensive, but it had the advantage that all advertising after that point reinforced the new global brand, not the old local one. The alternative is to try to transfer the old brand equity to the new gradually, without losing any value. This can be done by double branding (adding the new brand name to the existing packaging), which can help create allegiance to the new brand while retaining the attachment to the old. When Coca-Cola metamorphosed into Coke, the old brand's livery and packaging (and name) introduced the new brand. Now that allegiance has been so well transferred, the old name could conceivably even be dropped, if so desired. Where double branding is difficult or undesirable, the switch can be made—again in two stages—by dressing the old name in the new livery. When BP acquired Sohio service stations in the USA, the stations donned the green and yellow BP livery, but kept the Sohio name for a while, until the livery change had been accepted. Unilever has introduced a common, heart-shaped symbol for all its European ice creams, but is keeping the Algida, Langnese and Walls names in Italy, Germany and Britain, respectively.

STRATEGIC PRINCIPLES

Whichever approach is chosen to achieve uniform brands, key strategic decisions will be needed in the following areas:

Choose the right brands. This seems obvious, but may be the toughest decision of all. The crucial issue is whether the brand has staying power—whether it is the kind of brand that can be sustained and developed, over the long term, by an active program of innovation. Brand portfolio managers should look to the future and ask themselves which of their brands will be the strongest ten years hence.

Decide on the boundaries. In theory the global brand is the ultimate goal, but practical considerations may confine the scope of a brand to Europe or even a cluster within Europe.

Prepare a market strategy for the change. In a weak market, a full re-launch may be most effective, whereas in a strong market, double branding might be better. In both cases, the addition of a new consumer benefit helps, because it stimulates consumer trials, facilitating the transition.

Ensure scope for local adaptations. Uniform brands need not be insensitive to local tastes, if adaptations can be made efficiently. KitKat chocolate bars look the same all over the world, but the Malaysian bar has a different chocolate recipe that doesn't melt so easily, and in the Middle East, a three-fingered KitKat is marketed to match the value of a local coin.

Get the timing right. The success or otherwise of a double-branding brand change depends largely on judging correctly when enough brand equity has been switched to the new brand. Generally speaking, the longer the period of double branding the lower the risk of brand equity loss. So the earlier a program is embarked on, the better.

Anticipate pricing strategy. Because it is much easier to 'arbitrage' uniform brands (divert them from one market to another), manufacturers will come under greater pressure to price them uniformly. The advent of the euro has already made it much harder to sustain different prices within the euro-zone, and uniform brands make it harder still. It should be recognized at the outset, therefore, that a decision to embark on a European brand harmonization strategy creates an urgent need to address the issue of price harmonization.

PRICE HARMONIZATION AND THE EURO

The arrival of the euro as Europe's common currency has been both a blessing and a curse for multinational companies operating in Europe. It has been a blessing, because it has lowered transaction costs, eliminated currency risk and has made it easier to implement the supply chain rationalizations discussed in the next chapter. It has been a curse, because it has effectively brought an end to the era of lucrative price differentiation in Europe. Long-established price differences between countries of up to 100% on just a few 'cash cow' products, have been worth millions in profits to manufacturers. One major manufacturer of cleaning products calculated that lowering prices of a single key brand to the price charged in its most competitive European market would reduce its total European operating profits by 40%!

Price differences within Europe were already under attack, as pan-European buyers diverted products from cheap to expensive markets, but they had survived under a cloak of currency exchange risks, which the euro has removed. Must companies resign themselves to the disappearance of this lucrative source of profits? Many appear to believe so. Manufacturers introducing new products with standard European prices, welcome the decline in exchange rate distortions that the euro has brought. For established products, the situation is quite different. For these, manufacturers are carrying on, hoping that their price differentials can be maintained for a little longer, until the trade 'finds them out'.

TIME IS RUNNING OUT

The price differential window was closing fast before the arrival of the euro, as the rationalization and integration of their computer systems across Europe made the trade more conscious of national price differences. 'Parallel trading' (when goods are trans-shipped by retailers across borders) was on the rise, and retail chains were increasingly demanding common pricing. Differences in brand names and packaging no longer offered much protection. One manufacturer of specialty household cleaning products reported that customers were demanding common pricing, even when the brand name was different, because they knew the contents were the same. The ketchup of one global food manufacturer was routinely diverted from the UK to the higher-price Dutch market, despite the fact that the product's labels were in English and the taste of the Dutch formula was a little different from that of the UK product. Moreover, leading manufacturers were themselves increasing the awareness of price differences, by standardizing products and packaging to capture scale economies, and generating standard product images among consumers with pan-European advertising.

A PROACTIVE STRATEGY

There is a great opportunity for manufacturers to pursue a proactive strategy on pricing—and a great incentive too, given the money at stake. There are ways to limit the damage of price harmonization, and even ways in which companies can turn it to their advantage if they abide by the following key principles.

Negotiate from a position of strength. Because of local pricing discretion, retailers are often more aware of price differences than the manufacturers themselves. A survey by A.T. Kearney found that over 100 different types of discounts, allowances and special deals were in common use across Europe. Identifying them all can be a major project in itself. The first step is to integrate computer systems (no easy task for acquisitive companies), to improve internal price transparency. An ideal system would allow managers to obtain snapshot data on pricing instantly and directly from invoice data. If this is impossible in the short term, companies can start to get a rough idea about net prices in all their markets, by identifying and categorizing the types of discount and asking for local input about their use. The latter method needs very careful monitoring, however, because, as is the case with any information system, the quality of the output is dependent on the quality of the data input at local level. Sometimes, salesmen conveniently forget to report some of the 'extra' discounts they give during promotional campaigns, or they may be reluctant to refuse volume-related discounts when the volume targets are missed, or they may simply fail to provide updated information on a continuous and timely basis. Needless to say, the negotiation becomes quite one-sided when the retailer knows the manufacturer's cross-border pricing better than the manufacturer itself.

Develop a vision. Although senior executives of manufacturing companies welcome the impetus global customers can give to a distribution drive and value the savings associated with sending larger volumes to fewer distribution centers, they know that the larger the client, the more vital it is to their success. Being unlisted (or, worse, de-listed) by key clients, may make it uneconomic to buy the advertising needed to create brand awareness, and may thus reduce consumer demand to the point where other clients become dissatisfied. At the same time, regional managers and local salespeople tend to defend vigorously their local pricing discretion, because they have no incentive to take the broader view. Their sights have to be raised, therefore, which will require considerable investment in training and communications.

Moreover, the fact that patterns of trade inter-relationships are constantly shifting, as a consequence of acquisitions and expansion programs, means that the detailed implications of any pricing strategy are enormously complex. For example, the acquisition by French retailer, Auchan, of an equity stake in the leading Italian chain, La Rinascente, has affected the whole relationship between French and Italian retail markets. Markets that were quite independent are suddenly more closely linked, and customers' tolerance of price differences between them has decreased as a consequence. Developing a dynamic model, which spells out for everyone in the company the relationships that the top managers know are crucial, can help the whole company to identify the relationships and quantify them in terms of pricing strategy. This will enable the company to respond proactively to developments as they occur and get all the interested parties across Europe lined up behind a common European approach to pricing.

Know your limits. Armed with such a model, managers can then acquire a thorough understanding of price elasticity, by product and market. In the USA, a rule of thumb is that price differences tend to be tolerated if they do not exceed 7%. Manufacturers know that, if they exceed that limit, parallel markets will develop and 'diversion' will occur. In practice, of course, tolerance varies from product to product and market to market depending on such things as the degree of standardization and transportation costs.

Be proactive. Once tolerance levels are understood, and interrelationships have been assessed and tracked, a proactive pricing strategy can be developed. Manufacturers with a clear vision of where prices should be in the longer term across Europe will be in a position to start negotiations with trade customers, before such negotiations are forced upon them. Without such a vision they will have nothing to bargain about and will always be on the defensive. If it becomes clear that the price of a particular product in a particular market will have to be cut at some stage, there is much to be said for making a cut before the trade demands it. When linked to increased shelf space, promotional benefits and other favorable terms, which give the manufacturer an edge over its competitors, an early cut can increase market share.

THE TRADE-OFF

By meeting the big retailers half way with uniform brands and standard prices, manufacturers will win the chance to replace their traditional armed truce with their major customers with more constructive relationships. The short-term costs of such standardization may seem prohibitive, but in the longer term, manufacturers are likely to benefit greatly from closer, less adversarial relationships with their powerful retail clients. Manufacturers that fail to recognize price standardization is the price they must pay to enter 'win-win' games with the new breed of pan-European retailers are likely to be left out in the cold. Some manufacturers see this switch to uniform brands and standard prices as a job the current generation of managers can leave to their successors. But harmonizing brands across Europe or, better still, globally, will capture considerable scale economies and could establish a crucial cost advantage. If it is done gradually in a series of well-planned steps it need not be very risky or even very costly. Since it takes time to harmonize brand portfolios and prices, the sooner companies start, the better. History will not deal kindly with managers who leave this task to their successors.

10
An Integrated Supply Chain

A large, multinational manufacturer of food products has more than 100 plants dotted throughout western Europe, duplicating technology at many different locations. Since the fall of the Berlin Wall, it has added several more in central and eastern Europe to provide access to those markets and to the low-cost manufacturing opportunities they offer. It knows that it must rationalize its manufacturing, but what is the best arrangement, and how can support be mustered for change when plants still report to the country managers where they are located? The company also recognizes that re-configuring manufacturing is only part of the challenge it faces, and that it will not maximize the efficiency of its European supply chain, without a simultaneous rationalization of its distribution system.

In consumer goods industries, ECR (efficient consumer response) is yesterday's game. Today's imperatives in logistics are to explore new distribution channels, such as home delivery, the Internet and interactive multimedia, and respond to mounting competitive pressures by scouring the whole supply chain for cost cutting opportunities. In both manufacturing and distribution, the systems developed for a smaller, country-based Europe are rapidly becoming out-dated. They must be replaced by more efficient and far more flexible systems that are cheaper to run, and can respond more quickly to customer demands.

BEYOND NATIONALISM

Just as it is the theme of this book that Europe should cease to be seen as consisting of nation states, so it is the theme of this chapter that it is no longer appropriate to organize European manufacturing and distribution along national lines. Customs barriers are being rapidly dismantled, and in western Europe, at any rate, transport infrastructure has improved so much, that it is now entirely possible for a Spanish plant to supply the Swedish market efficiently, and vice versa. Moreover, tastes are converging across borders as freer trade brings more choice, to more customers. Italians have acquired a liking for duvets from their northern neighbors, and the British have developed such an appetite for Belgian chocolate that UK supermarket chain, Sainsbury's, sells it under its own private-label.

But a glance at an average multinational's European factories and warehouses reveals that very little has so far been done to reflect this steady convergence of tastes in manufacturing and distribution arrangements. The main reason for this tardy response is that there is a lot of inertia in these systems. Closure and relocation costs appear to managers with local mandates and relatively short-term perspectives, impossibly high, compared to likely benefits. In Spain, laid off workers demand to be paid over 45 days' wages for each year of employment, and then there is the cost of dismantling and relocating, or writing-off fixed assets. In addition, optimal production and distribution arrangements for western Europe can quickly become distorted and cluttered by a few acquisitions. The rush to take advantage of market and manufacturing opportunities in central and eastern Europe is complicating matters further. But managers with broader perspectives know that, in the long run, the economies of scale of a modern European supply chain will far outweigh the costs. In this chapter, we will look at how managers should tackle this dauntingly difficult and very expensive exercise, starting with manufacturing.

RATIONAL MANUFACTURING

Experience has shown that there are six secrets of success in the rationalization of manufacturing:

Centralize supervision. Country managers have no incentive to take a continental view so they should not be responsible for factories. At Kimberly-Clark, manufacturing is managed on a pan-European basis. Some products remain market-specific, and are still made locally, but more and more are being sourced from plants supplying the entire European market. At Unilever's Home and Personal Care division, all detergent plants report to the same senior vice president.

Take stock of existing plants. Assess each plant in terms of a comprehensive set of criteria including:

- ***Optimal distribution radius*** (see Figure 10.1). Clearly this is shorter for toilet paper, than for toothbrushes. It is also shorter for plants in Russia, and other eastern European countries, where the transport infrastructures are relatively underdeveloped, than for plants in Belgium.
- ***Capacity.*** Do not measure this on the basis of one shift a day five days a week. Manufacturing rationalizers should think of capacity in terms of three shifts a day for at least six days a week.
- ***Optimal size.*** In large factories using many technologies, the costs of increasing complexity quickly outweigh the economies of scale. Generally speaking, in factories employing more than 500 people it is difficult to maintain the personal relationship with each factory worker that is needed to ensure his or her full commitment to the success of the plant, both in terms of output and of quality.
- ***Proximity to materials and components.*** The cost of a product is often heavily influenced by the landed cost of components and materials, so sites close to major suppliers and ports of delivery should score high on those counts.

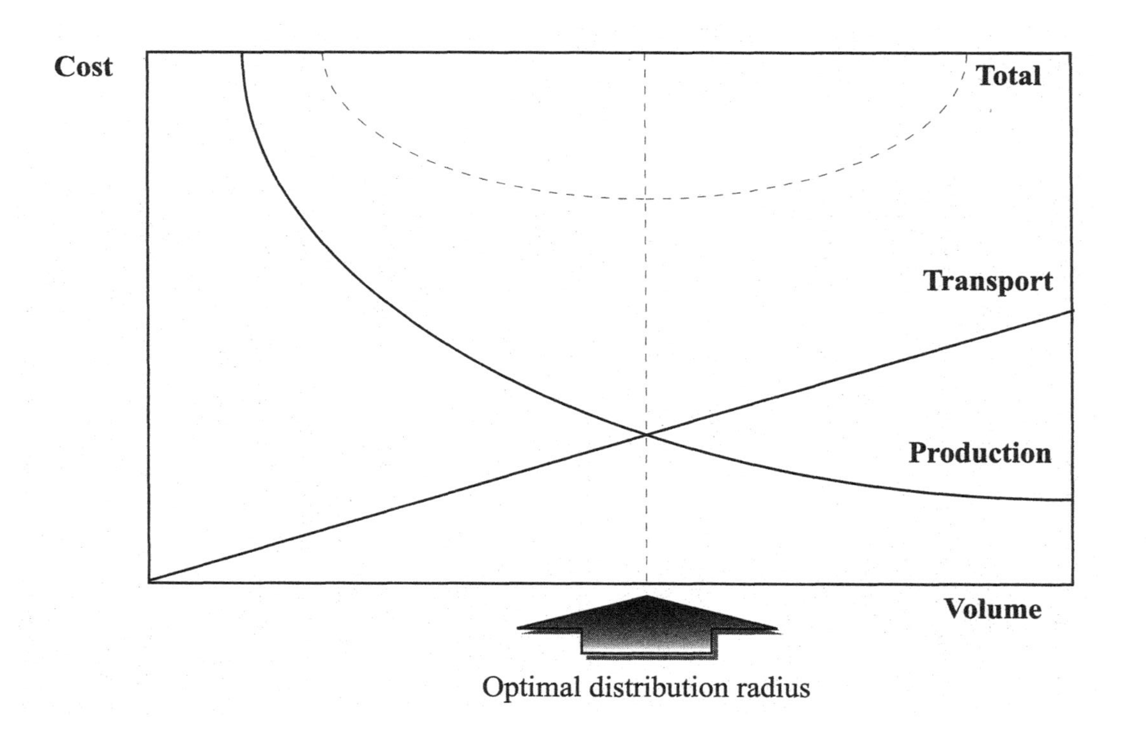

Figure 10.1 Total delivered cost

- ***Tax and duties.*** Although corporate tax rates still vary among EU member states, and many trade barriers to, from and within eastern Europe remain, tax rates are converging fast and most eastern European countries now have association agreements with the EU, establishing tight timetables for the elimination of quotas and duties.

Assume one plant per technology is ideal and more than one has to be justified. This is clearly a very reasonable assumption from the capital investment and overhead containment points of view, because more than one plant duplicates capital spending, maintenance, support facilities and supervisory management. If duplicate plants seem to be needed, it will be much easier to assess the economic case for them when the above analysis of existing plants has been completed.

Adopt uniform brands and products, wherever possible. A single plant for the whole of Europe can handle some local variations, but managers should question whether such local variants are really necessary. One food manufacturer blends its tomato ketchup, to reflect alleged local taste variations in each European country. However, as indicated in Chapter 9, one large Dutch retailer is in the habit of 'diverting' the UK ketchup blend to its stores, to take advantage of UK price promotions, and there is little sign that Dutch consumers notice any difference.

Take account of labor costs. The fact that German manufacturing labor rates are now seven times those in the Czech Republic (see Figure 1.1) is clearly of the utmost significance particularly for the manufacturers of labor-intensive products. As Volkswagen has proven, lower eastern Europe wage rates represent a great opportunity to reduce manufacturing costs, not just because the labor is skilled, as well as inexpensive, but also because it is close to western European markets. Luigi Maramotti,

CEO of the Max Mara Fashion Group, points out that the company's production planning and quality control center in Hungary, is closer to group headquarters in northern Italy than a similar center in southern Italy. But major investments are needed to exploit these differences in costs, so it is important to consider how durable they are likely to be. As Europe becomes more integrated, labor rates and other cost factors, such as labor laws and regulations, will converge.

A phased approach. Closing plants is not only painful and very disruptive to the organization—it is also very expensive. There is much to be said, therefore, for a phased approach that will minimize the costs and risks of closing or relocating production. In his book *Dual Restructuring*, Fritz Kroeger describes a three-step process to minimize risk, once a decision has been taken to relocate production to a lower labor-cost country. First, transfer simple, labor-intensive assembly processes, and import raw materials and components. Next, phase in some locally sourced components and raw materials. Finally, when the results are satisfactory, transfer the manufacture of the complete product line. That is easier said than done, of course. In practice, the schedule will have to take account of local interests, and the intense emotions aroused by plant closure plans. The rationalization of manufacturing is as much about psychology and politics, as about economics, but multinationals have no choice but to respond to the growing pressure to increase their efficiency by cutting the number of plants, even while adding more through acquisitions, joint ventures and start-ups. A company disciplined enough to see every plant as dispensable, unless proven otherwise, has a major advantage over its less focused competitors.

One example of such an approach is SC Johnson Wax. In the early 1960s, when duties still existed among members of the then European Common Market (ECM), but were due to disappear within a few years, the company decided to close all the ECM factories and supply the whole market from a single plant located in Holland. "We achieved significant economies of scale that put us well ahead of our competitors, planting the seed of our success in Europe," said chairman Sam Johnson.

But manufacturing is only part of the equation. The costs of distribution from the factories to the customers need to be tackled too, and customer service also needs to be improved.

OPTIMIZING DISTRIBUTION NETWORKS

An A.T. Kearney survey of 1,000 European companies, reveals that the average logistics cost of finished products amount to roughly 10% of sales. Some companies are struggling with ratios twice that, but the 'best-in-class' have already shaved their logistics costs by a third or more. Those who lag behind in modernizing distribution systems will find themselves not only at a considerable cost disadvantage, but also at a service disadvantage from the point of view of internationally-minded trade clients. Major retailing chains, such as Tesco, Carrefour and Metro, are demanding logistics systems that can deliver flawless orders, lower inventories, instant replenishment and total integration, via EDI, all on a pan-European scale. As if that were not challenging enough, the eastwards expansion of Europe's boundaries is complicating logistics enormously. The relatively poor state of the transport infrastructure in much of eastern Europe, the persistence of customs borders and, in some countries, limited currency convertibility, have obliged many companies to rely on local distribution arrangements for the time being. Eventually of course, the continuing need for ever greater efficiency will require such local systems to be integrated into a single, pan-European distribution system.

At Case Corporation, a leading US manufacturer of agricultural, and construction equipment, CEO Jean-Pierre Rosso is re-shaping the industry worldwide by re-engineering the company's supply chain, from suppliers through manufacturing and distribution, to customers. Inventories have been halved, and both Case and its distributors are getting their cash earlier. "Our ultimate goal," says

Rosso "is to reduce the impact of the business cycle on the company."

Savings associated with faster inventory turnover are usually the most immediate benefits from improved distribution. Other savings can accrue from fewer order errors, faster payment of invoices and reduced transportation costs, because of fuller trucks and fewer one-off emergency shipments. These and more general economies of scale can keep transportation costs down even though the distances covered rise. Not all logistics overhauls work as well as Case's, however. Common errors include trying to improve too many parts of the supply chain at once or, conversely, changing one part without having first devised a complete plan for all the changes that will ultimately be needed. Another recipe for disaster is to go ahead without the full commitment of all affected parties in the organization right up to board level. And finally, too many companies still believe that it is enough to invest many million of euros in an integrated software system.

Experience suggests that the following lessons should be borne in mind when determining the scope of any distribution system rationalization.

Take a pan-European view. Service requirements differ from customer to customer, but don't need to vary by country, so review the managerial structure. Do regional distribution centers report to a central supply chain vice president, or to the country managers where they are located? If the latter, how can regional distribution center managers be seen to be impartial when tough rationing decisions have to be made as they inevitably do from time to time?

Define the parameters of the project very clearly. Identify the different processes in the supply chain that need to be re-engineered, and analyze them. Look at the distribution end of the chain from a service perspective. What does the customer really want and need? Do a benchmarking analysis not only against competitors, but also against the best-in-class in other industries.

Determine the locations and number of distribution centers. This is a crucial and complex decision which will depend on the optimal delivery radius of the products, as well as the service needs and locations of clients. In eastern Europe it will probably entail a two-stage process involving several local distribution points, to start with, which may then be rationalized once customs borders have been dismantled and transportation infrastructures have improved.

Do not underestimate the information technology (IT) element. IT makes the pipeline transparent. Depending on the service objective, it can include the implementation of EDI with customers, automatic stock replenishment, automatic picking and packing right up to a full just-in-time system, going all the way back to sourcing with EDI links to both suppliers and customers.

Decide whether all this should be done in-house, or whether it could be outsourced. More and more firms are choosing to outsource logistics to pan-European providers. Alternatively, a network of outside suppliers is complex to run, but reduces dependency on a single supplier.

The 'stages of excellence' concept is helpful in defining how far the distribution system needs to be changed. Henner Klein and Hans-Stefan Hascher, of A.T. Kearney, devised Figure 10.2 to illustrate the potential benefits of a more efficient, and more responsive distribution system.

A world-class distribution system will meet the current needs of customers, at minimal cost to the supplier, and anticipate future changes in distribution channels and buying patterns. Many companies are already responding to the rapidly changing patterns of distribution in Europe. Bed linen manufacturer, Zucchi/Bassetti, for instance, has noted that the number of specialist shops selling

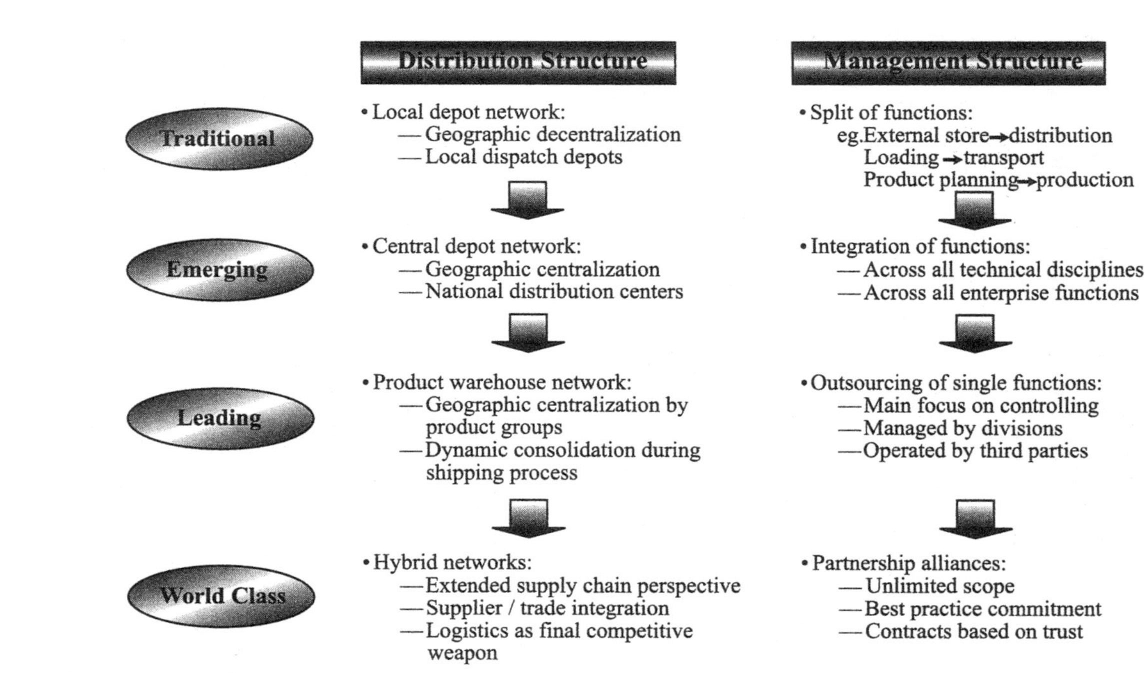

Figure 10.2 Stages of development

its products is gradually declining, but department stores are not increasing their market share at a corresponding rate. The Milan-based company is therefore experimenting with distribution outlets in furniture and home furnishings stores. Other companies, such as Gillette, are exploring Internet selling channels.

The emphasis, in modern consumer goods logistics, is shifting from the store shelf, to home replenishment, and all major consumer goods manufacturers should be exploring the opportunities and threats associated with this development. The first priority for manufacturers, however, is to optimize their conventional logistics systems. Those that can distribute efficiently and flexibly, and provide a high level of customer service, at a low cost through their existing channels, will be best placed to lead the way to the logistics of the future.

WORKING THE CLUSTERS

It seems likely that within a decade or so, the best European supply chains will bear little resemblance to those of today. Manufacturing seems certain to migrate eastwards, as low-cost ex-Soviet countries take the lion's share of new capacity, while distribution arrangements will be progressively re-configured to reflect the convergence and 'clustering' of tastes. It should be remembered, however, that the easterly migration of labor-intensive activities will itself help to eliminate the differences in labor cost that now commend it. Economics differences will gradually narrow, and so become less important factors in determining the most appropriate locations for factories and distribution centers. Enlightened multinationals will look beyond existing economic differences and construct their supply chain visions within a more durable segmentation of greater Europe. For in the long run, it will be the kind of 'zoological' clustering described in the first six chapters (Bees, Gazelles, Storks and Bears) that will shape the markets of greater Europe.

11
The Continental Back Office

As companies re-think their approach to the changing European market, restructuring the back office (finance, IT, HR and administrative support) has, until recently, tended to take a back seat. Some multinationals are now beginning to realize, however, that the answer to the mystery of why their European operations are seldom as profitable as their US operations, despite achieving the same ratios of sales to marketing, sales forces and logistics, lies in the back office. Tax is a factor, particularly in Germany, Italy and France, but at the pre-tax level, a higher overhead is the main explanation for lower European profitability. The point was forcefully brought home during the frantic Year 2000 (Y2K) systems conversion. The need to adjust up to 15 separate country systems in Europe begged questions about the costs of the 'local adaptability' allegedly provided by maintaining full management teams in every European country. If a general manager, an accounting department and a dedicated IT system are needed in each European country when US operations can get by with a district sales manager in each region, it is no wonder European overheads are higher.

The opportunity for substantial overhead reduction is not the only reason why back office rationalization should be seen as an integral part of a European re-structuring project. It is also a pre-requisite for improved customer service and other front-end improvements. Manufacturers will be unable to satisfy global clients demanding more centralized European services, without integrated

IT systems that facilitate accurate and customized responses to client needs. Just-in-time production, automated replenishment, and growing competitive pressures to react instantly to the latest market information, require better communications and data access at a time when technological advance is constantly extending the boundaries of economic feasibility. A bonus for many firms is the opportunity modern IT offers to improve internal services by capturing, managing and disseminating marketing, sales and other useful information with data warehousing. Such systems will not be possible, however, until information is standardized and apples can be compared to apples. While different costing systems produce different costs and spawn different policies on discounting and advertising allowances, manufacturers will be unable to gather consistent information directly from invoicing data, and the ideal of a pan-European pricing policy will remain a dream out of reach, with costly consequences (see Chapter 9).

An A.T. Kearney benchmarking study on the finance functions of leading companies revealed considerable scope for cutting costs in finance processes and improving levels of service to the customer. Possible cost reductions were as much as 35–45% (see Figure 11.1), indicating a short payback period. "For many companies," says author Dr. Theo Klein "the administrative function is so little rationalized that it resembles a car factory, before the invention of the assembly line."

The advent of the euro is concentrating minds on back offices just as powerfully as a while back did the Y2K conversion. When French clients were billed in francs and Italian clients were billed in lire, it was natural to have separate invoicing functions in each country. Now that most European clients are billed in euro, it is hard to justify anything more than an accounts receivable section for each country, and there is no reason why it should be located there. The French or Italian client can call a local number, and be answered in perfect French or Italian by someone located in a country, such as Ireland or Britain, where wage rates and payroll

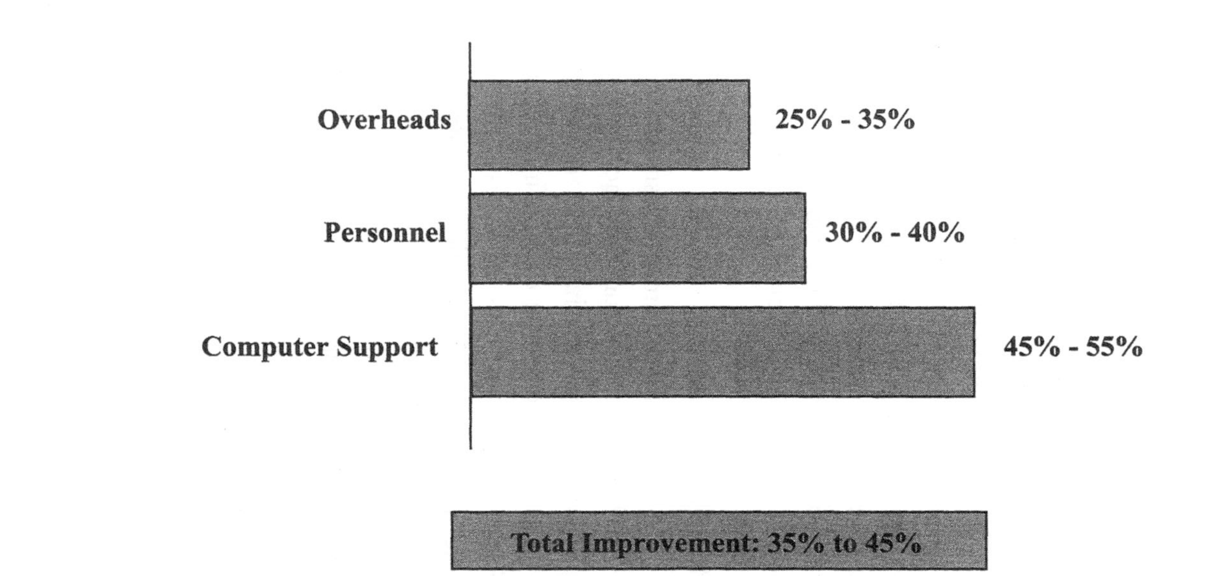

Source: A.T. Kearney Benchmarking database

Figure 11.1 Percentage reduction from shared services by cost component

taxes are low, and where there are plenty of foreign language speakers. For example, the Belgian customers of an industrial perfumes manufacturer still get support with a local call, but it is now answered by a native Belgian, based in The Netherlands.

Despite the euro, European back office re-structuring will remain a feasible but challenging task because although successive EU directives have harmonized accounting requirements in many areas, separate reporting is still required for national payroll and tax purposes. In addition, labor laws vary, language differences remain, and most manufacturers have an incompatible multitude of legacy IT systems built up nationally or inherited through acquisitions. The expansion of Europe complicates the picture further.

OVERCOMING THE OBSTACLES

For these reasons, a well-planned and comprehensive approach to rationalizing finance and administrative functions across Europe is crucial. A broader perspective is needed that seeks answers to basic questions, such as 'what is the real role of the finance function nowadays?' In leading companies it plays an increasingly strategic business advisory role, in addition to its traditional 'controller' role. IT needs and objectives must accommodate such developments. Given the rationalization objectives for other operations (see earlier chapters), firms need to ask themselves what processes are involved, what decision support systems are needed and what communication channels will be used.

The following is a brief summary of a well-tested methodology for back office rationalization.

Take a comprehensive view. This may seem obvious, but it is well worth stressing. Taking the time to step back and review the scope and priorities can clarify the processes and costs involved. Start by asking which finance and administrative activities must be performed close to that function's customers, and which need not. Certain functions long considered local by necessity, can now be performed remotely. Other previously local functions now have to be centralized, to meet customer demands. At Seagram, for example, a global 'key accounts' group co-ordinates strategy, negotiations and customer service for its increasingly global customers. What kind of administrative support does this group need? And where should this support function be located?

Since IT systems can be expensive, companies need to be clear about what IT they need. A full EDI system may seem desirable, but will cost several orders of magnitude more than an e-mail based system. There has been much talk recently about the value of 'data warehousing', but bitter experience has shown that without careful planning and piloting, data warehouses can turn out to be far more trouble than they are worth. Modern communications media are strong productivity enhancers for all multinational companies. Voicemail, e-mail and video conferencing reduce travel costs, and increase the number of people who can attend meetings.

Benchmark costs against rivals and best practice companies. Look at the leading companies in other industries, as well as competitors. Benchmarking is essential because cost reduction programs need realistic targets. Compare the ideal with the achievable. A single European service center may be the ultimate goal for the finance function, but is it practical? A European company that has grown mainly through acquisitions could have several hundred accounting groups in Europe, so it would be very hard to consolidate them all at once. A more practical approach is to begin by shifting transactions processing to one country, then consolidating some services by cluster, and ultimately moving a few processes into a single centralized pan-European shared service system (see Figure 11.2).

This approach is also suitable for IT and communications, but in these cases, it is important to anticipate future demands, when making initial systems investments. The location decisions for the centralized services must also be realistic. The ideal location is where

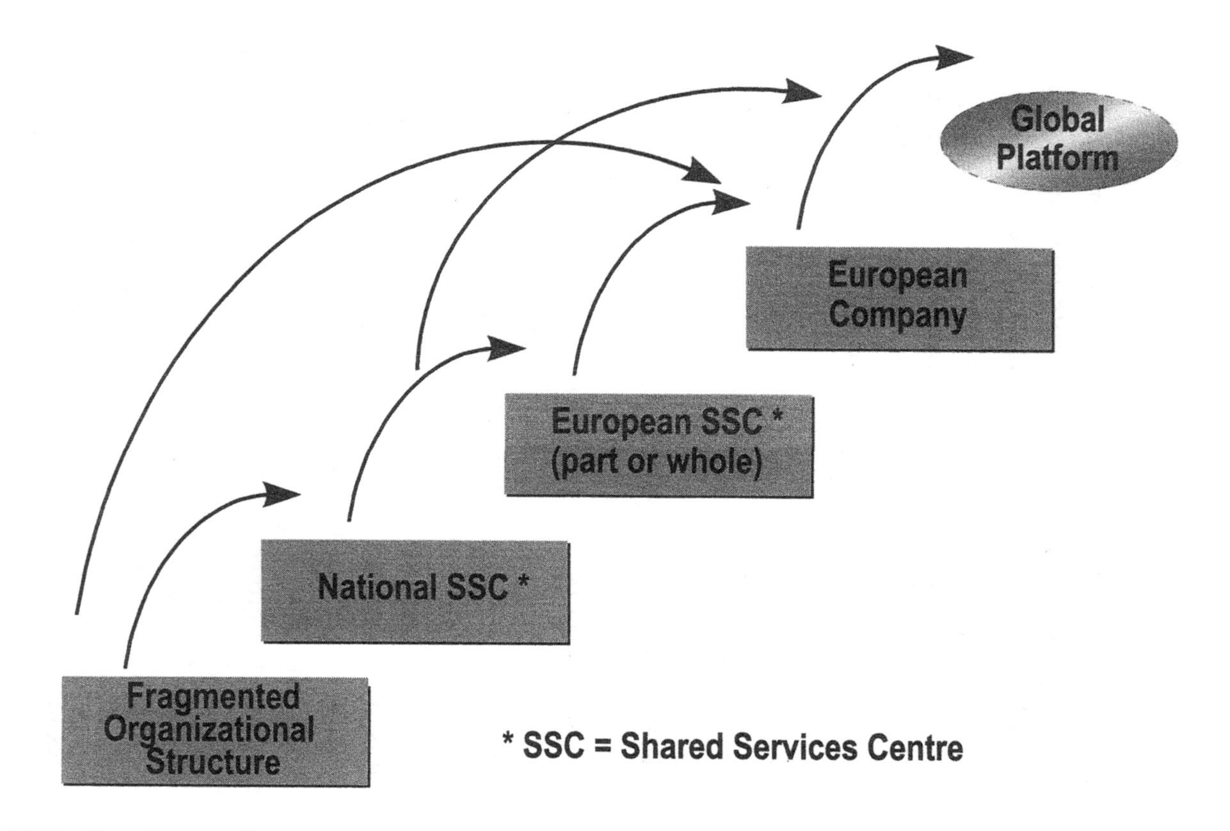

Figure 11.2 How far to go?

accounting, IT and language skills are available at low cost, and communications infrastructures are efficient. This is why the Storks are popular locations for multilingual call centers. The existing distribution of 'back office' resources and the needs of important customers must also be taken into account, when choosing locations for shared services.

Standardize processes, to prepare for rationalization. This may involve re-designing some processes, 'cleaning' data and running pilots, to test proposed changes. And, given the far-reaching implications of back office rationalizations, it may also be necessary to develop implementation, and training guide-lines, and detailed HR plans.

Decide which processes to outsource. Companies, such as Time-Life Books and Rolls-Royce have begun to outsource processes, such as payroll, billing and customer queries, they would not have dreamed of entrusting to a third party just a few years ago. Specialist process suppliers are taking over, not just the processes themselves, but also the equipment and staff associated with them. They can do the job more efficiently, because they can capture economies of scale not available to their clients and can nurture expertise and offer career development paths in activities, which are 'core' to them, but peripheral to their clients.

With the groundwork laid, pilots successfully completed, and everybody 'on board', a gradual rollout of the rationalized system can begin. But note the key word, 'gradual'. More than a few major projects have foundered even at this late stage, because the rollout was too ambitious. The trick is to work on a few processes at a time, and only embark on the next few processes when the earlier changes have proved manageable.

In restructuring the European organization, a single back office becomes a powerful enabler, because it lowers the overheads, provides comparable information throughout the organization, and allows the local managers to focus all their attention on serving the needs of the local customers. In addition it provides organizational flexibility: entering or exiting markets only requires the establishment of a front office capability interfacing with the client, and a physical delivery capability, which is often, at least initially, contracted out. That is why so many companies are considering it. To achieve pan-European economies of scale, however, a second powerful enabler is needed: a pan-European corporate culture.

THE PROBLEM OF PAROCHIALISM

Well into the 1990s the goal of most European managers was to rise to the top of their national subsidiaries, and then make them the most successful and powerful local organizations in the corporation. This suited their employers fine, because in those days, success came from the deep penetration of largely independent local markets. Since then, many companies have gone through several waves of re-structuring, but managers' goals have hardly changed. This parochialism of European managers is a major obstacle in developing an efficient, flexible, pan-European business. Successful national subsidiaries run by local nationals have constantly resisted attempts to centralize manufacturing, R&D and customer service, both for fear that it would erode their power base and because of their genuine belief that only they really understand how to succeed in their markets. When these changes are imposed despite their resistance, local managers lack the commitment and incentive to make them work, and thus they fulfill their own negative prophecies. Most international companies recognize this parochial outlook is inefficient, not only because it denies them the economies of scale they are so anxious to capture in their increasingly competitive markets, but also because it makes them resistant to change. Some leading companies have gone one step further, and recognized the vital role HR management can play in widening managerial horizons.

Seagram, for example, has tried hard to change its culture so that it can embrace change, and adapt continuously. As Martin Frost,

Seagram's European CEO, explained: "If we can create a culture of continuous improvement and re-engineering, it will generate process innovation by stimulating the creativity of the people operating in this fluid environment." But how? How to change the mindset of often entrenched middle and senior managers, without wholesale firing and re-hiring that would not only be highly disruptive, but could also result in key skills being lost to the organization? By not expecting too much too soon, for one thing. Changing a culture requires consistent and sustained communication, and a lot of patience. More specifically, it requires action in four crucial areas of human resource management.

Recruitment. It's essential to take the long view. By hiring multicultural or, at least, adaptable MBAs, to work in countries other than their own, the company starts to build a pan-European culture from the bottom up. This may not pay off immediately, but the longer it is delayed, the longer it will take. Younger people are preferable, because they tend to be more mobile, and less costly to relocate. This is particularly true of people from eastern Europe who graduate from a western business school. Intelligent, eager to learn 'western' ways and often much less expensive then their western counterparts, they should be trained in western subsidiaries to take over the job of running eastern European operations a few years later.

Training. But what of the existing cadre of middle and top managers? In consumer goods, especially foods, there's a bias in favor of native local managers, because of the value of their intimacy with, and sensitivity to, the local culture. How can they be induced to adopt a broader perspective, and make a commitment to the European or global parent organization?

This can be done by temporarily assigning some local managers elsewhere to immerse them in the broader corporate culture, or by bringing in expatriate managers to broaden the horizons of local

	Math		Science	
1	Singapore	643	Singapore	607
2	South Korea	607	**Czech Republic**	**574**
3	Japan	605	Japan	571
4	Hong Kong	588	South Korea	565
5	Belgium (F+)	565	**Bulgaria**	**565**
6	**Czech Republic**	**564**	Netherlands	560
7	**Slovakia**	**547**	**Slovenia**	**560**
8	Switzerland	545	Austria	558
9	Netherlands	541	**Hungary**	**554**
10	**Slovenia**	**541**	England	552
11	**Bulgaria**	**540**	Belgium (F+)	550
12	Austria	539	Australia	545
13	France	538	**Slovakia**	**544**
14	**Hungary**	**537**	**Russia**	**538**
15	**Russia**	**535**	Ireland	538
16	Australia	530	Sweden	535
17	Ireland	527	United States	534
18	Canada	527	Canada	531
19	Belgium (W+)	526	Germany	531
20	Thailand	522	Norway	527
21	Israel	522	Thailand	525
22	Sweden	519	New Zealand	525
23	Germany	509	Israel	524
24	New Zealand	508	Hong Kong	522
25	England	506	Switzerland	522
26	Norway	503	Scotland	517
27	Denmark	502	Spain	517
28	United States	500	France	498
29	Scotland	498	Greece	497
30	**Latvia**	**493**	Iceland	494
31	Spain	487	**Romania**	**486**
32	Iceland	487	**Latvia**	**485**
33	Greece	484	Portugal	480
34	**Romania**	**482**	Denmark	478
35	**Lithuania**	**477**	**Lithuania**	**475**
36	Cyprus	474	Belgium (W+)	471
37	Portugal	454	Iran	470
38	Iran	428	Cyprus	463
39	Kuwait	392	Kuwait	430
40	Colombia	385	Colombia	411
41	South Africa	354	South Africa	326

Source: 'World Education League' – The Third International Maths and Science Study TIMSS)

Figure 11.3 13-year-olds' average score in TIMSS (international average = 500).

staff, or both. In eastern Europe, such horizon-broadening programs require particularly skillful management, but in most central and eastern European countries, there is no shortage of highly-able local talent. In a recent standardized test, conducted in 41 countries, six of the top 15 places in both math and science were taken by eastern European countries, with the Czech Republic second after Singapore in science and sixth in math (See Figure 11.3).

This local talent has to be trained, however, particularly in marketing and selling techniques. A few local managers can be temporarily assigned elsewhere in Europe, to be immersed in the corporate culture and approach. However, for the rest training must be done locally, and given the high quality of trainees, by very talented trainers. "We need to find capable trainers, willing to be assigned, sometimes, to a difficult location," says Jean Martin, head of Unilever's operations in central and eastern Europe. "Even for an organization as large as Unilever, this is a major challenge. And because of the high quality of the local people, a foreigner who is not very good will quickly lose credibility with the employees that need to be trained."

Training existing managers in more established markets can be tricky, too. McDonald's 'Hamburger University' was started in Chicago in the 1960s and most large corporations in the USA have such courses. Now DaimlerChrysler and British Aerospace have set up their own 'corporate universities' in Europe, and several major companies have developed executive training programs that focus on European issues, in association with leading European business schools. This helps to create a European management mentality, and also an informal network of European middle managers.

Incentives. The obvious way to persuade managers to take a 'broader' view is to alter the bonus systems so that bonuses are partly, or even mostly, linked to Europe-wide performance rather than to that of their local organization. Be wary of over-complicating the incentive system, however. This will distract management from focusing on a few key, attainable goals.

A matrix organization (in which a manager has simultaneously both responsibility for a local organization and pan-European responsibility for a product) should be used sparingly and with caution, but it can help lift managers' horizons, open windows for the cross-pollination of ideas and show everyone that a non-national can make useful contributions to a local market. Matrixing is best treated as an interim measure, however, as a step towards a pan-European organization, the top team of which is staffed by nationals of all European countries, not only by natives of the country where the headquarters are located.

Communications. Language plays a crucial role in creating the framework for a European structure, and English is the obvious choice for the 'official' language. If English is not the official language, the size of the available pool of top talent to recruit from is much reduced. It is estimated that a fifth of the world's population speaks some English, two-thirds of scientists work in English and English is the dominant Internet language. But although many multinational companies have chosen English as their working language, the rule is rarely enforced. This constrains management choice, and de-motivates managers whose native language is not the company's de facto, top management language. It also hinders efforts to rationalize other processes in the European organization. For example, efficient communications can be blocked, simply because e-mail messages not written in the official language cannot be so widely forwarded.

Regularly exposing local managers to the reality of other European markets is also very important. At Merloni, one of the leading European makers of white goods, the top 15 local and corporate executives participate in a management board that is involved in all major operating decisions. This board meets at different locations throughout Europe. "People in different countries will continue to have different ways of thinking, different values and different languages," says CEO Francesco Caio, "but giving our senior managers a broader view of the company helps create consensus, while a very diverse executive group makes better decisions."

Finally, no company should underestimate the power of top management, particularly the CEO, to set the tone and spread the European message. Formal newsletters, covering topics of European interest, can be valuable, but less formal, instant means of communication, whether it be e-mail or fax, are more influential. Companies can save money, by eliminating glossy newsletters that arrive too late, and spend it on making sure that information flows fast and frequently.

In short, top managers should use every opportunity to spread a pan-European message. Experience has shown that getting rid of parochial attitudes is a slow and difficult process, and the evidence suggests that the multinationals that prospered most in the age of localism will find it particularly hard to achieve.

12
Conclusion

There are two aspects to the European challenge. The first is the challenge the enlargement and integration of Europe poses for Americans: they have to come to terms with their loss of economic dominance, as Europeans had to come to terms with the shift in economic power described by Jean-Jacques Servan-Schreiber 30 years ago in his book *Le Defi Americain*. It will not be easy for them, but it is a necessary adaptation that is becoming urgent.

Some commentators who had been skeptical about EMU saw the euro's early weakness as a vindication, but exchange rates have nothing to do with economic power. They reflect interest and growth rate differentials, and it so happened that America's economy was growing faster than Europe's in early 1999, and US interest rates were relatively high: hence the westward move of 'hot money' across the Atlantic. A more significant development in 1999 was the euro's instant dominance of bond markets. In the first quarter of 1998, bonds denominated in ECUs (European Currency Unit, pre-cursor of the euro) accounted for less than 15% of the international bonds issued, against the US dollar's 40% (see Figure 12.1). In the same period of 1999, euro-denominated bonds accounted for 45% of bonds issued, against 44% for the US dollar. A currency that can instantly wrest market leadership in the bond market, from one that has been the world's reserve currency for half-a-century, is no weakling.

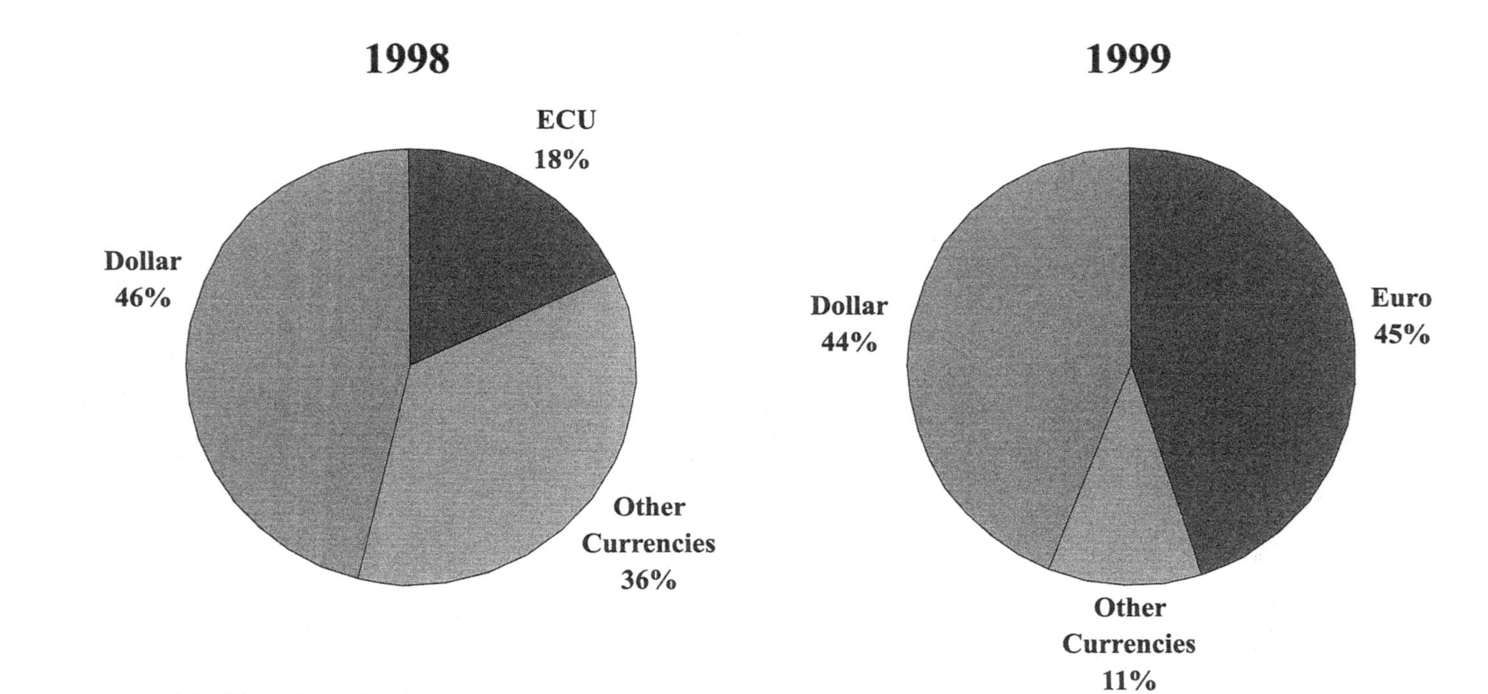

Source: Capital DATA Bondware - first quarter

Figure 12.1 The euro has become the leader in international bond issues

The other aspect of the European challenge is the challenge the enlargement and integration of Europe poses for firms that plan to operate throughout Europe, which this book is designed to help them address. They need to re-organize themselves and they need to do it soon, because the leaders in the Europeanization process will have a significant competitive advantage over the laggards. North America has been used, in this book, as a model for the development of clusters, and the proposed organizational approach to the European market is also 'American'. A California-based company would not consider setting up new factories or separate invoicing centers when expanding into Texas or New England if it has excess capacity in California. Such an approach would now be equally inappropriate for UK-based firms trying to expand on the continent, or French firms trying to enter the German market, and vice-versa. All companies established in or planning to enter the European market should re-organize or organize themselves to take advantage of the greater economies of scale offered by the single market, the euro and the integration of the eastern European markets.

The fact that the most appropriate organizational model for greater Europe is American means that, the psychological challenge apart, the re-organization task should be easier for American than for European firms. US multinationals are used to organizing their domestic operations in a centralised way similar to the one outlined in Figure 7.4. They do not have to un-learn the out-dated national model of organization that has been common in Europe until now. They can distinguish the wood from the trees more clearly than their European counterparts. They are better prepared, in other words, for the challenge and therefore have a chance to strengthen their positions in greater Europe, as greater Europe's position in the world economy strengthens.

The rise of greater Europe is an historic challenge for multinationals. Indeed it would not be stretching the point to say that responding to it is the single most important task facing managers of all companies that are already or aspire to become multinational. The passing of the baton of economic dominance is a rare event, and offers companies which understand its importance and have the will to adapt to it quickly and appropriately, an enormous and unique opportunity to steal a march on their competitors.

Bibliography

Anthony Beevor: Stalingrad – Penguin Books, 1999

Norman Davies: Europe – A History – Oxford University Press, 1996

Francis Fukuyama: *The End of History and the Last Man,* Free Press, 1992

Joel Garreau: *The Nine Nations of North America,* Houghton Mifflin, 1981

Dr. A.H. Heineken: *The United States of Europe*, Amsterdam, 1992

Will Hutton: *The State We're In*, Jonathan Cape, 1995

Paul Kennedy: *The Rise and Fall of the Great Powers*, Random House, 1988

Pieter Klapwijk: *Global Economic Restructuring*, Klapwijk Holding N.V., 1996

Fritz Kröger: *Dual Restructuring*, MacMillan, 1996

Adam Smith: *An Inquiry into the Nature and Causes of the Wealth of Nations*, 1776

The Economist Pocket World in Figures, 1999 Edition

Lester Thurow: *Head to Head. The Coming Economic Battle Among Japan, Europe and America,* Warner Books, 1992

Paul Valéry: *Collection Bibliothèque de la Pléiade*, 1957

Hugo Young: *This Blessed Plot,* MacMillan, 1998

G. Zhukov: *Reminiscences and Reflections*, Progress Publishers, Moscow, 1985

John Zysman and Andrew Schwartz, Editors: *Enlarging Europe: The Industrial Foundations of a New Political Reality,* University of California at Berkeley, 1998

Index

Printed and bound by CPI Group (UK) Ltd, Croydon, CR0 4YY

23/04/2025

14660944-0001